More Praise for *Dare*

"*Dare* will give you that push we all need from time to time, showing you how to excel by believing in yourself, acting boldly, and being unafraid to take risks."

—Carole Hyatt, bestselling author,
and founder and CEO, The Leadership Forum

"Are you still waiting to be noticed? Stop it. Becky Blalock shows you how to overcome the single biggest thing that holds women back: fear. Read *Dare* and learn how to boldly seize the reins of your career, and your life."

—Lisa Earle McLeod, author, *Selling with Noble Purpose*

"Becky has assembled a treasure trove of practical, well-illustrated advice, from communication techniques to getting valuable personal feedback to negotiating salaries and much more. Her personal stories are supplemented with research and vignettes from other successful executives. A valuable book for every woman in business!"

—Martha Brooks, retired president and COO,
Novelis, Inc., and board member, Bombardier,
Harley-Davidson, and Jabil Circuit, Inc.

"Looking for something to help you tackle a challenge in your career? In *Dare*, you will find the encouragement and coaching you need to believe in yourself and challenge the status quo. Successful women share their stories of lessons learned, and practical advice is given to provide you with the confidence to tackle anything. Everyone's journey is different. Learn from the best, apply it to your situation, and enjoy success."

—Mylle Mangum, chairman and CEO, IBT Holdings, and
board director, Reynolds Metals Company, Haverty Furniture
Companies, Barnes Group, Express Inc.,
PRGX Global Inc., and Decatur First Bank

"Top leadership in corporate America is no longer a lofty goal for women. *Dare* is full of wisdom from great female leaders who help you understand how you, too, can reach your full potential."

—Susan Stautberg, cofounder and cochair,
WomenCorporateDirectors, and president, Partnercom

"Becky has been a leader in the United Way movement as well as in business. She has brought her full experience to this leadership book by women, for women. It has taken years to reach a point where there are enough women in senior roles to model the way for others, and *Dare* contains priceless wisdom from some of the most accomplished women of our time. Their lessons learned and success strategies will boost your confidence and challenge you to achieve more."

—Cynthia Round, executive vice president,
United Way Worldwide

"*Dare* is an excellent resource for any professional woman. Becky's practical and insightful advice will give you a clear path to the top."

—Kathy Ameche, author and traveler-in-chief,
womanroadwarrior.com

"Becky Blalock has risen to the very top of the male-dominated information technology industry. She is a national treasure. *Dare* is simultaneously inspirational, informational, operational, and recreational. A must-read for future leaders of every gender."

—Thornton May, futurist; author, *The New Know*,
executive director, IT Leadership Academy

DARE

Straight Talk on Confidence, Courage, and Career for **WOMEN IN CHARGE**

BECKY BLALOCK

JB JOSSEY-BASS™
A Wiley Brand

Published by Jossey-Bass
A Wiley Brand

One Montgomery Street, Suite 1200, San Francisco, CA 94104-4594—www.josseybass.com

Jossey-Bass books and products are available through most bookstores. To contact Jossey-Bass directly call our Customer Care Department within the U.S. at 800-956-7739, outside the U.S. at 317-572-3986, or fax 317-572-4002.

Wiley publishes in a variety of print and electronic formats and by print-on-demand. Some material included with standard print versions of this book may not be included in e-books or in print-on-demand. If this book refers to media such as a CD or DVD that is not included in the version you purchased, you may download this material at http://booksupport.wiley.com. For more information about Wiley products, visit www.wiley.com.

Library of Congress Cataloging-in-Publication Data
Blalock, Becky, 1955-
  Dare : straight talk on confidence, courage, and career for women in charge / Becky Blalock. — First edition.
    1 online resource.
  Includes index.
    Description based on print version record and CIP data provided by publisher; resource not viewed.
    ISBN 978-1-118-74465-9 (pdf)—ISBN 978-1-118-74473-4 (epub)—ISBN 978-1-118-56264-2 (hardback)
  1. Women executives.   2. Leadership in women.   3. Success in business.
4. Businesswomen.   5. Career development.   I. Title.
  HD6054.3
  658.4′094082—dc23   2013028525

Printed in the United States of America
FIRST EDITION

HB Printing   10 9 8 7 6 5 4 3 2 1

CONTENTS

In memory of my remarkable mother: Dorris Faulkner Bradford

In honor of my remarkable daughter: Alexandria (Alex) Nicole Blalock

In recognition of remarkable women everywhere

FOREWORD

By Anne Mulcahy

Former Chairman and CEO, Xerox Corporation

W hen Becky approached me to write the foreword to *Dare: Straight Talk on Confidence, Courage, and Career for Women in Charge,* I was thrilled. She and I share a strong desire to mentor the next generation of women leaders in business. We know how critically important it is to learn from others, through their successes and their failures. There's no magic wand for leadership, but there is much to be taught and much to be learned, and what Becky has learned and is now about to teach will greatly increase your chances of rising through leadership positions and succeeding in each of them.

I first met Becky when she was the CIO of Southern Company and a big Xerox customer. In one customer visit, she asked if I would be willing to meet with the executive women of her company and talk about my career journey. I was honored to comply. Later, we met again when I was the keynote speaker for the Georgia CIO Leadership Association. These two meetings revealed to me the breadth and depth of Becky's generous and collaborative spirit. I'm excited but not at all surprised that she is now extending the reach of her generosity through this wonderful book.

Becky understands that what we women leaders most need is the willingness to take risks. Too often too many of us just don't have the self-confidence—or the support!—to step out of our comfort zone and tackle new challenges. Yet, of course, it is these very challenges that help us grow from one stage of our career to the next. Even more important, it is through these challenges that we grow the companies we work for.

My own experience echoes and affirms so many of the lessons you will find in this book. I have seen the stark necessity of effective leadership in times of crisis and prosperity. Many of us remember the Xerox of the 1990s, when it was an unrivaled icon of operational expertise. When I began my tenure as president and COO in May 2000, however, we were facing some real problems. I can't think of a time in my career when leadership was more important. I saw that our company had two major assets: great customers who didn't want the brand to die, and a committed workforce who didn't ask me, "When will we be closing our doors?" but instead asked, "What will we look like going forward?"

I took these as the positive signs they were, and I took them also as a call to leadership. As Becky says, leaders need to have a clear vision, set clear objectives, align their organization, and communicate like crazy. One of my mentors told me, "When things are good, talk about what needs improvement. When things are bad, talk about when they will get better." Just as Becky advises here, we took some big risks, and we made tough choices. We restructured, and we sold businesses not core to our future. We partnered with others to use our internal talents better. In 2002 we lost almost $300 million, but in 2006 we made over $1 billion.

Becky stresses the importance of being grateful for what we have and making sure we leave a legacy. I subscribe to her call to action. On my retirement, I also decided it was time to give back, and I took on the role of chairman of the board of trustees for Save the Children. I now use the great experience I gained in corporate America to help this wonderful, vibrant organization address the needs of children challenged by poverty.

Effective and bold leadership is every bit as important today as it was back in 2000. The demand for it will only increase in years to come. Every person who reads this book has the opportunity to make a commitment to leadership that will have a positive impact on her organization, her team, and her career.

You need to embrace the challenges in front of you. Don't wait for change or for someone to hand you an opportunity. Follow Becky's priceless advice: look for needs, create opportunities, then take the risk and step confidently into leadership. Those in the generation behind you need your success, and those of us who have gone before are rooting for you. Read on—and learn from the best!

DARE

FOLLOW ME

I n 1978 I began my career at Georgia Power, and I worked for the next thirty-three years in the Southern Company system. Until 2011 I was senior vice president and chief information officer, directing IT strategy and operations across the 120,000 square miles and nine subsidiaries of Southern Company. I led more than 1,100 employees in delivering information technology to one of America's most respected companies. I had a guiding hand in executing over a billion dollars in the new technology initiatives that repeatedly earned Southern Company recognition as one of the "100 Most Innovative Companies" from *CIO* Magazine and also a spot on *Computerworld*'s "100 Best Places to Work in IT" list.

Three-plus decades doesn't seem such a terribly long time when you're the one who's lived them, but, in terms of women in business, it's practically an eternity. When I started out, most women went to college to become nurses or teachers or, let's face it, to find a husband. Although nursing and teaching are great professions—and there's nothing wrong with finding a husband, either—I soon realized that women could also do great things in a host of occupations traditionally associated with men: as doctors, attorneys, accountants, and, yes, business leaders. Of course, back in the 1970s, few women majored in business. I was one of only a handful in my program at the University of West Georgia. When I went to graduate school at Mercer University in 1984, I saw a few more women around me, but not many.

The women of my generation fell prey to the discouraging myth that "women can't do math," and math is essential if you're going into business. But even bright women I knew who *did* excel at math—and *knew* they excelled at it—didn't pursue a business career. Of my closest friends, not even one considered going into the business world.

So how did I end up there, holding C-level positions at one of the most successful companies in the nation?

I learned early how to dare.

My dad was a sergeant in the U.S. Air Force, and we moved, well, a lot. I attended eight elementary schools, three junior high schools, and four high schools. Over the years, many well-meaning friends and colleagues have shaken their heads with sympathy when I've mentioned this.

"It must have been tough," they said. "How could you possibly have adjusted?"

Maybe being an Air Force brat *was* tough sometimes, but I don't remember it that way. What I *do* remember is that being the new kid just about every year I went to school made me stronger—or at least made me *feel* stronger, which may well amount to the same thing.

As the perpetual new kid, I realized I had a choice. I could keep my head down and my mouth shut in an effort to blend in, or I could dare to introduce myself, to raise my hand in class, and to generally make myself known. It took some confidence and some courage to do this, but with each and every move to a new town and a new school I discovered inner reserves of more confidence and more courage. Each time I dared made it easier to dare the next time. It was like working a muscle, developing it, making it stronger and more reliable with use.

A young life of one new situation after another was not the only thing my dad gave me. He was always a good listener and adviser, but he was absolutely adamant about two things: *don't* smoke, and *do* go to college. He didn't care what my sister and I chose to study or how we paid for it. Both were up to us.

An Air Force sergeant doesn't earn a fortune, and I didn't have much cash for college. One semester, I worked a retail job, making $1.65 per hour. When a marketing professor approached me to get my help with a market research study and said he would pay me $5.00 for every survey I was able to collect, I jumped at the opportunity. I did not have money, but I did have friends, and I knew my friends would take the survey. After I collected the surveys—and my fistful of fives—he asked me to help him analyze the data. I agreed, and I quickly learned that I had quite a knack for data analysis, taking a large amount of information and seeing the trends within it. The professor advised me to major in marketing, saying, "You would excel in the field."

Maybe all those years I spent choosing to dare made me especially receptive to those three words: *you would excel.* In any case, I chose to dare again, and that is how my journey toward business began.

As the years passed in a career marked by relentless change, my daring became the true constant and secret of my success. My willingness to step into positions in which much was unknown, to open my mouth and speak up, to innovate and push unpopular agendas—all these "dares" led to my biggest wins and ultimately made me a successful executive and leader.

C-SUITE OR BUST

I've written this book for any woman looking to lead in corporate business, or contemplating the idea. But even more specifically, I've written it for the woman in middle management who is wondering how to make that climb—difficult for anyone, but really hard for women—to C-level management. Although mid-level managers are critically important to business, and although the job can be rewarding, for a certain kind of woman even a very good middle-management slot begins to feel like a hole, and she begins to feel stuck. I've been in that hole, and I'd like to give you a hand up.

As a former CIO I'm still part of an all-too-small group: corporate women who made it to the top. As of 2012, women made up 46.9 percent of the U.S. labor force and 51.5 percent of "management, professional, and related occupations."[1] Impressive—and yet, at the *very* top, in executive leadership positions, women are still in the minority. In 2012 women made up 14.3 percent of executive officers in Fortune 500 companies, up from 14.1 percent in 2011. And they held 16.6 percent of Fortune 500 board seats in 2012, up from 16.1 percent the year before.[2]

I would never argue that senior leadership is for every woman, and I can't answer the question of why so few women have broken through that glass ceiling. I'm not a scientist or a sociologist; I'm a businesswoman. I learned my own lessons on the way up, but perhaps more important, I managed and mentored hundreds of men and women as a senior leader in my company. In doing so, I saw how the most successful employees positioned themselves to climb the corporate ladder. I also watched as many others either backed away or tried but fell short—and much to my distress, all too often it was the women.

There are many obstacles to reaching the executive suite. The senior executive women I interviewed for this book pointed to a shortage of executives, male and female, willing to advocate on behalf of rising women, and although they stressed the importance of taking "stretch" assignments, those roles that push you beyond your current expertise, even at the risk of failing, they also admitted that few executives—again, male or female—were willing to give these opportunities to rising personnel, especially young women. Of course, it is just such assignments that prepare us to reach the top rungs on the corporate ladder.

Yet, precious as the stretch assignments truly are, many women lack the confidence to seize them when the rare opportunity arises. They fear they are not ready for the assignment or the move, or they are reluctant to take on controversial issues. Faced with a choice between middling comfort and risky opportunity, they often choose to stay where they are. Rather than "lean in," in the now-famous coinage of Facebook COO Sheryl Sandberg, too many step back and assume that diminishing their career or working independently are the only ways one could possibly balance work with a satisfying family life.

For some women, stepping back is the right choice, and I applaud all those who make that choice consciously. This book is for those women who are all-in, determined to become part of that select upper echelon of corporate leadership and share the job of determining the direction and success of the largest economic engines of our time.

DARE TO LEAD

Continuous career advancement happens only when you dare to take risks, and what I've seen myself and heard from other women *and* men is that men seem to have a leg up compared to us when it comes to this particular arena.

Over and over again, as I interviewed successful senior executive women for this book, asking them why they thought there were not more women in jobs like theirs, I received a variation of the same reply: *women need to be more open to new opportunities; to take more risks; to say yes, even when they're unsure.*

Women need to dare.

I know from personal experience how frightening it can be to venture into a new role that takes you far out of your comfort zone, the intellectual region in which you feel yourself to be an expert. But I also know from that experience—know absolutely—that we grow most when we personally feel most at risk.

At one point in my career I had what I then considered a "dream job," assistant to the CEO. This wasn't an administrative position, it was one of the roles the company used to groom high-potential leaders. I was the first woman in the role, and it made me part of the executive team. Whenever the CEO couldn't attend a meeting, I was sent in his stead. Finally I had a window into the company at a strategic level, and I was learning everything I could. One day the CEO came into my office and said that he and the executive committee had met and decided I would be a good fit for a brand-new job they were creating. It was regional chief information officer, with responsibility for running the IT function of several subsidiaries and reporting up to the enterprise CIO.

I almost fell out of my chair. My training and my career background were in accounting, finance, and marketing. As for computers, I didn't know anything except how to use one—and sometimes I needed help with that. But, then, how do you say no to the CEO? So I swallowed, grinned broadly, and instead of falling out of my chair, popped up from it, took his offered hand, and thanked him for the wonderful opportunity.

That's what I *did*. What I *felt* was great fear of failure and a tremendous amount of self-doubt. It even occurred to me: *this might just be the end of my career*. Yet I decided to accept these feelings, painful as they were, and simply set about establishing goals and learning the new job.

Several times in my career I would be asked to take assignments in areas in which I had neither deep knowledge nor real experience. Fortunately for me, I quickly realized that in these situations the job was always more about leadership and an ability to be flexible and learn and grow than it was about the technical particulars. I was shocked one day when a young woman on my team, a woman who had worked with me in a prior role, told me, "You are a better leader in IT than you were in accounting."

"I'm the same person now as I was then, so how can that be?" I responded.

"You built a lot of the processes in accounting, and you were the technical expert," she explained, "so there was a real tendency for you to get into the detail and try to manage everything. Here in IT you are truly leading instead of managing."

It was then that I realized just how powerful this assignment was in building my leadership skills and making me a more confident leader. The job I thought would ruin me had instead brought out my best work. After a short time, when I moved to yet another job, I did so with the confidence that I could add value even—maybe *especially*—in areas in which I was not a subject matter expert, as long as I had a clearly defined vision. I learned to surround myself with smart, talented people and to trust them to execute on our shared initiatives.

Making that first tough developmental move had been a critical step in my career. Several years later, the enterprise CIO position opened up. Never mind that it was a job several levels higher than my position level at the time; people remembered the great work I had done in my short time as a regional CIO, and I was promoted to this senior role in the C-suite. Had I turned down the earlier move to regional CIO, this opportunity would not have been offered to me.

Even if you're still unsure about whether you're cut from the right cloth for the executive life, today you'll find that the mind-sets and skills of daring are essential for any career path. It is more important than ever to venture into new roles that take you far out of your cultural and intellectual comfort zone. In today's rapidly changing professional and technological worlds, you cannot afford to be an "expert" in a narrow field.

The broader context is liable to change right out from under you. When things move fast in business, you need to take the broadest possible view. If you don't, the targets will shoot clear out of your constricted field of vision. Taking the broad view means moving into new areas all the time and proving you can learn fast and lead others.

PREPARE TO DARE, TOGETHER

Today it is more important than ever for us as women to be able to match our male colleagues in the ability to step up and dare to risk; to say *yes* even when we know for a fact that we don't yet know everything we'll need to know to follow through. If you're doing this, it will not just be for you—or even for the sake of our gender. Getting the new female majority to step up and lead is critical to our nation's competitive future. As Saadia Zahidi, head of the World Economic Forum's Women Leaders and Gender Parity program, once said, "Women make up one-half of the brain power of the human capital that's available to an economy."[3] We need all the trained, experienced, and capable brain power available if we are to continue to grow economically. We cannot compete if more than half our workforce does not feel fully empowered to succeed.

A generation or two ago, women had only a few career choices open to them. On occasion, particularly determined women would be allowed to share the man's world of work—but typically in a subordinate role, such as that of stenographer or secretary. When World War II took the men to battle, women left their cash registers and typewriters to labor in war plants and other traditionally male work environments. The world's eyes were suddenly opened to what women could accomplish if given the opportunity. The airplanes, ships, tanks, guns, and munitions those women made enabled America to win a world war.

My generation made the next big leap, demanding equal opportunity in the workplace and slowly but surely proving to our male bosses that we could be more than secretaries and typists. A few of us even went all the way to the top. In doing so, we helped improve economic conditions in the United States, adding 25 percent to our gross domestic product since 1970.[4]

We've come so far, but we're not done. A new generation of women, supported by men at home and at work, needs to dare to break through that final glass ceiling to the C-suite.

This book is designed to help develop the character, skills, and relationships to prepare you to swallow your fear and take the leap; to dare boldly and unapologetically when those career-defining moments arise; to dare even bigger than I did.

The dozens of senior executive women from some of America's most respected companies whom I interviewed for this book are trailblazers, too. They have shared their personal stories of how they dared to take on challenging assignments and how they found the self-confidence and courage to do it. They've also opened up about how they recovered from mistakes.

They have accomplished great things in their respective careers and paved the way for the next generation of women leaders. I hope you will be as inspired by them as I am. The great success they enjoy is possible because of the courage and self-confidence they have—but underneath it all, they too have had to overcome fear and uncertainty. They have all made mistakes, and they are all better and stronger leaders because they learned from them.

These women are also passionate about helping other women. Anyone who says women don't support and help each other speaks from ignorance. The "Queen Bees" of the past are not the women (or men!) who succeed in today's business environment, and they certainly won't get far in the future. The most successful leaders are those who "pay it forward," and the women I interviewed are all great models of just that. They are from diverse industries and have very different backgrounds, but they are exceptional leaders and superb examples for us all.

Wherever you are in your career, mentors are essential to helping coach you through your journey. Through this book, I'd like to stand among them.

Let this book serve as a guide while you dare to take on new challenges, and let it help you understand that in taking them on, you are not alone. I'm asking you—as a woman in business, in leadership—to do what so many find it most difficult to do: dare to believe in yourself and take risks, and take them routinely, over and over again.

CHAPTER ONE

DARE TO SET THE TARGET HIGH

Harmonize Vision and Values

I always wanted to be somebody, but now I realize I should have been more specific.

LILY TOMLIN

Anna Maria Chávez, CEO of Girl Scouts of the USA, is the daughter of immigrant farm workers from Mexico. She was born south of Phoenix, Arizona, in a tiny town where the per capita income is $9,194 and the largest employer is the local prison.

Nevertheless, early on in high school Anna decided that she was going to go to Yale. "You're a Latina, don't you think you should stay in state?" people asked her. She ignored them and set about doing the things she needed to do in and outside the classroom to make her dream a reality. "I was like, 'Wait a minute, I have no boundaries!' I was determined to wind up at Yale, and I did."

In 2013, as the first Latina to lead the Girl Scouts, Anna displays boldness and clarity of vision that have never been more important as she works to update and evolve a hundred-year-old organization so a new generation of girls can dream even bigger than she did, and "become leaders of their lives, families, communities, and businesses." Alongside her goal of making sure the organization directly meets the needs of the young it serves, her vision is to make Girl Scouts the leader in a nationwide conversation around girl leadership and women's roles in society.

Where do you get the skills to see the future with crystal-clear vision, as Anna did from such a young age and continues to do today at Girl Scouts? The best executive leaders see the future so vividly that they can make it real for others while they map the path to get there. Once you move out of middle management and into the executive suite, you're no longer working toward the goals of others. You set the agenda. Weeks or months may pass without input from, or even contact with, your boss. To flourish, you need to have both the courage to dream big and the practiced ability to paint the vision clearly and engage others in the plan.

BELIEVE YOU CAN GET THERE

To get to the executive suite, women need strength of vision that exceeds men's. We have to earn the right to be seen as leaders because worldwide the notion of ideal leadership is still biased toward men. For example, a 2006 Catalyst study surveyed 935 alumni of the International Institute for Management Development.[1] People from different regions identified a number of different skills as most important to leadership, but unanimously found men to be better at whatever skill they selected. In the United States and England, for example, respondents listed "inspiring others" as most important to leadership, and then rated women as less adept at it than men.

When I started out three decades ago, few women were in senior roles in the corporate world, so what *seemed* obvious—self-evident, even—was that the barriers holding us back were permanent, natural, and forever. Unmovable.

Today, however, many have broken through. Though they may be in the minority, women do hold senior leadership positions in every major industry. And yet a 2011 McKinsey study concluded that a disproportionate number of "bright, highly-motivated women at middle management levels—and higher—[frequently] turn down opportunities for advancement, look for jobs outside their company, or leave Corporate America altogether."[2] Chief reasons cited included women's fears that they wouldn't be able to manage a family and an executive career; the concern that embedded institutional mind-sets still bar women from leadership roles; and a general lack of satisfaction with their chosen profession.

Even seemingly positive words—*balance, sacrifice, ambition, happiness*—can affect our attitude and keep us from exploring

The Leaky Pipeline

A 2011 McKinsey study found a "leaky pipeline" of women to the executive suite: in 2011 women held 58 percent of undergraduate college degrees and represented 53 percent of new hires, yet held only 37 percent of mid-level management positions, 26 percent of VP positions, 14 percent of SVP positions, and only 3 percent of CEO roles.[3] Women in the study reported "specific barriers . . . that convince them that the odds of getting ahead in their current organizations are too daunting," including:

- *Lifestyle issues.* "Many women expressed a concern about the always-on 24/7 executive lifestyle and travel requirements."
- *Embedded institutional mind-sets.* "Managers (men and women) still tell diversity officers that 'Everybody "knows" you can't put a woman in that particular slot.'"
- *Embedded individual mind-sets.* "Women are, on average, less satisfied than men with their chosen professions and jobs . . . [and] as women get older, their desire to move to the next level dissipates faster."

our full range of possibilities. These words and the cultural myths into which they're woven are powerful, but only because we ourselves endow them with power by letting them define our stories.

It's so easy to let our vision be defined—and limited—by others. Perhaps you've heard that elephants, despite having legs like tree trunks, can be tethered by a stake in the ground barely bigger than a pencil, simply because as babies they learned the painful way that the stake would hold them. Once they believe the tether holds, they never try to escape it.

Each of us needs to make sure that none of the tethers that still hold us back are self-imagined—and to dare to take that final leap.

MAKE YOUR PERSONAL VISION SPECIFIC

To be a woman aspiring to a top leadership position, you've got to dare to go beyond the circle that's been inscribed for you. And you've got to develop a sense of vision so strong, so clear, so audacious, that when people either subtly or explicitly tell you that a certain cherished goal is a fantasy, you ignore them and go to Yale anyway—or whatever your equivalent is to Anna's brass ring.

I have mentored and coached many women over the years. What continues to surprise me is how many times I have an initial meeting with someone and she can't tell me what it is that she wants. You might think this is a problem limited to young women, but I see it in many who are mid-career as well. It is very hard to coach someone for success when she herself has not defined what success looks like to her. When I get a vague or noncommittal response from someone, what I'd like to say is, "Well, my crystal ball isn't working very well today."

There are many aspects of your career that people can help you with, but defining what you want is something that only you can do. You can seek counsel and ask others' advice, but in the end it's up to you to determine what you want.

I know I can't be too critical here, because I wasn't always certain of what it was that *I* wanted. I believe I could have been more successful earlier if I had been more strategic about what I wanted and how I was going to get there. It is a great moment

The Mentors Speak: On Vision and Values

My grandmother instilled in me a sense of determination, a belief that all of us have an imaginary train track inside of us and our job in life is to stay on that track until we arrive at our destiny, no matter what it takes. Throughout life, you'll encounter people and events that will try to knock you off, but you have to fight with every fiber of your being to stay on that track.

Anna Maria Chávez, CEO,
Girl Scouts of the USA

Anything is possible. I am an example of that. Adapt the goal when you have to, but don't give up on it. You may not have it all in the timeline you planned, but anything is possible if you work hard, prepare hard, and never give up. Find your mentors, and find your advocates in all areas of your life.

Veronica Sheehan, SVP,
*Global Network Operations
and International IT,
Turner Broadcasting System*

Spend time to assess your value system, align career and life choices to those values, and live every day in a way that when you go home and look in the mirror, you can say, "I was *me* today." These are the most important steps to building self-confidence. They also eliminate the risk of having to decide who you are in any given circumstance.

Lyn McDermid, CIO, *Federal Reserve System*

when you realize that your sense of being tethered is just that— *your* sense, rather than an absolute reality. But what use is pulling up that stake and freeing yourself if you have no idea where to go?

"Where there is no vision, the people perish," goes one of the proverbs in the Bible. That's a very old piece of wisdom, and I wish someone had reminded me of it early in my own career.

Don't make the mistake of thinking of *vision* as something soft or impractical, reserved exclusively for poets, artists, or inventors. *Vision* is about being perfectly clear about what you want to achieve and why, to the point of being able to picture yourself having done it. It's daring to let yourself think big, beyond the next step, looking toward a whole career or an entire life. *Vision* is about setting goals that are both intensely meaningful to you and bigger than you think you can achieve.

DARE TO WRITE A PERSONAL VISION STATEMENT

Your personal vision statement describes what you want your life and career to look like in the future. Developing one at every stage of your career—in fact, annually—not only will help propel you to the top but also will prepare you for the unique challenges of executive leadership. Once you understand what you want, you can then create an action plan to get yourself there. There are others who have accomplished what you desire, and they can show you the way. But the first step toward self-belief is self-clarity, possessing a clear vision of what you want in your life and career.

Why is putting your vision in writing so important? Two-thirds of your brain are involved in processing visual information, such that writing something down is the closest equivalent to using a zoom lens for your brain. Shifting your vision from "idea" to "object" makes it more real. It allows you to reflect on it and develop it—and, perhaps most important, to share it. As a leader, your effectiveness depends on not just seeing the future but persuading others to see it as well.

The beauty of having a vision statement is that it can be your guide through both your work and your personal life. It allows you to prioritize where you invest your time. It helps you know when to say no to things that don't fit your plan. It can also act as a yardstick against which you can measure the current situation and your progress. Reread your most recent plan frequently, remembering that every time you do, you further embed it in your memory and are better able to visualize making it happen.

My own vision statements have changed over time. Yours will, too. I have developed mine using the values that that are important to me. I'll share them:

Fifteen years ago:
I will be a senior leader in my company who has a reputation of delivering results with integrity and helping people around me succeed in their personal and professional lives. I will keep myself fit and healthy and seek constant learning. My faith and family will be my top priorities.

Today:
I will make all decisions in my life through the lens of my faith, stay healthy and focus on the needs of my friends and family, and enjoy life while finding ways to help others.

Your vision should be flexible enough that it doesn't bind you when a great opportunity comes along. You need to be ready to adapt as situations change or new information becomes available. That's the funny thing about leadership:

you have to see the goal, but be able to dodge and pivot like an Olympic soccer player as conditions change over time.

For example, although it's not explicit in my vision statement, writing this book is part of delivering on my personal vision. I've learned a lot about being successful in life, and I am trying to help others by passing it on.

Vision statements are like road maps. They need updating because there are always new roads being built. Some roads may make the trip faster or more enjoyable, but each new path must be carefully evaluated according to what you want in your personal and professional life.

Once you've crafted or updated your vision statement, you should put together a more detailed plan of steps you'll take over the next months and year to get there. This is the moment to describe your goals as specifically, objectively, and even quantitatively as possible, because this gives you a clearly defined target to shoot for and helps you translate thoughts and dreams into the actions necessary to transform them into reality.

As you move forward in your career, there will be times when your vision clouds. Moments of tedium and stress can challenge your desire to continue pressing forward. Roberta Bondar, Canada's first female astronaut, told me that at one time she had reached a point in the space program when her passion dulled and it began to feel like a "job."

"When I was actually in space, I floated over to the window to look down at Earth," she told me. "While looking through that window I began to think about when my sister and I played space games as children. We used to put sheets over the furniture and pretend we were in a spaceship. I thought about all the things that went into helping me get to where I then was, in that moment. That helped me regain my vision."

Fortunately, you don't need to go all the way to outer space to refocus yourself. Looking back and reflecting on all you have accomplished—and all those who have helped along the way—can quickly bring your vision back into bright, vivid focus.

CORE VALUES:
YOUR VISIONARY GPS

Although our vision will change over time, our values tend to stay the same. Core values serve as an infallible GPS that guides our vision by defining our internal conduct as well as our interactions with others. They give us the courage required to make even the most difficult decisions, those that ultimately define our career.

When Beverly Daniel Tatum was offered the chance to join the running for the presidency of Spelman College in Georgia, she almost turned away from it. It was a giant leap in responsibility and would mean moving to a new state, which would require interrupting her husband's career and yanking her son out of his high school. The position would take her way outside of her comfort zone, make her the public face of an institution, and give her work not just regional but national significance. "There were many good reasons to stay put in Massachusetts," she says.

But then, during a visit to the campus to help her decide, she picked up a brochure and read the school's mission statement: "An outstanding historically Black college for women, Spelman promotes academic excellence in the liberal arts, and develops the intellectual, ethical, and leadership potential of its students. Spelman seeks to empower the total person, who appreciates the many cultures of the world and commits to positive social change."[4]

"Excellence, leadership, empowerment, appreciation, and respect for others—these five values have been at the core of my personal and professional work for my entire career," says Beverly. "I could not imagine a better or more concise statement of what is important to me. When I read these words, I knew what I should do."

Back at home, she shared the brochure with her husband, who responded by saying, "If you don't pursue it, you will always regret it." As a family, they agreed that if she were to be selected as president, her son, David, and husband, Travis, would remain in Massachusetts for two years, for David to finish high school and for Travis to become eligible for state retirement benefits.

"The prospect of the separation was daunting, but we decided to move ahead," she says. "That visit to Spelman College convinced me that I could make a unique and meaningful contribution to higher education and the world by leading this institution, which had such a powerful mission so in tune with my own values. For all the reasons that made me initially

The Courage to Lead a Nation

Laura Liswood, cofounder of the Council of Women World Leaders, interviewed fifteen elected heads of state and leaders of government, including former British prime minister Margaret Thatcher.[5] Her interviews with these individuals provide some great insights into the nature of women's leadership and confidence. Liswood discovered that although the female leaders varied in many respects, they had four characteristics in common:

- *A diverse view of the world.* They understood what was happening within their country, what was happening globally, and where their country fit.
- *Courage and conviction.* They were willing to take risks and challenge the status quo, honoring tradition but never believing that everything *had* to be the way it was. Their role, as they saw it, was to prepare for the future.
- *Excellent communication skills.* First and foremost, they were great listeners. They sought feedback from a wide range of constituents before they delivered their succinct and powerful messages.
- *Spiritual grounding.* Although they had different religions and faiths, their spiritual orientation guided them, especially during the most difficult of times.

hesitant, I felt nervous about my choice, but at the same time, I reflected on the words of a pastor friend who told me, 'God will not lead you where God cannot keep you.'"

A Survival Guide for Tough Decisions

Whether we realize it or not, we all have core values. They influence our feelings and determine our priorities. Once you're an executive, you'll be asked to develop a vision that serves the broader direction of your company. How you accomplish that vision, however, is almost entirely driven by your own value system. Because you serve as a role model for everyone you lead, your values will cascade down through the organization. So remember, this isn't just about staying true to your own beliefs. Leadership presents the opportunity to make an impact beyond your immediate reach.

The difficulty lies in that not all core values are created with full consciousness, which makes it easier for us to trip ourselves up in aligning vision and values. There's a serious practical danger here. When we set goals that are misaligned with our values, our motivation to act on those goals wanes quickly; likewise, when we make decisions that "just don't feel right," our ability to follow through successfully is severely handicapped. Intrinsic motivation—when we're propelled by desire from within—leads to much more successful outcomes, according to Heidi Grant Halvorson, author of *Succeed: How We Can Reach Our Goals.*[6] Finally, misaligned values affect our ability to lead others. People are less likely to trust us when they sense that we're being inauthentic and lack confidence in our mission.

Being more deliberate and more conscious about how you formulate your core values is essential to setting you on the right path to achieve your personal and professional vision. For one thing, conscious work around identifying values helps ensure that these values are truly yours—*chosen* rather than merely absorbed from your environment without reflection or reason.

Thoughtfully defined, your core values work in harmony with your vision to outline, quite vividly, just what it is you want to do, and then dramatically improve your planning and follow-through over time. They allow you to create a career of your own choosing rather than a course determined by the decisions or prejudices of others.

More immediately, values help you in everyday decision making, particularly when decisions concern your relationships. If you create a strong set of core values, you will find that when you honor them, you will feel—well, you feel a deep sense of satisfaction, even when decisions are difficult and make some people unhappy.

Being clear on core values helped Carol B. Tomé navigate one of the most challenging assignments of her career successfully: serving as the CFO of The Home Depot during the worst recession in the United States since the Great Depression. Between 2006 and 2009 the company lost $13 billion in sales. As the business contracted, the leadership team had to make some tough decisions, including closing stores, exiting certain lines of business, and reducing 10 percent of the company's support staff. Carol was asked to analyze the situation and make these recommendations, and was charged with communicating the company's actions and their financial implications to the world.

"All of our decisions as a leadership team were guided by our company's core values, which stress taking care of associates, customers, communities, and shareholders," says Carol. "When you stay focused on your core values, the decision-making process is straightforward. Because of this, I never lost sight of my responsibility to these key groups, especially our associates. I realized that they were all counting on me, and that I couldn't let them down."

The need to downsize was a fact, not something that Carol could control. What she could control was how they did it. "For instance, when we decided to close our Expo business, I visited the impacted stores and talked to both customers and associates about our decision," she told me. "I wanted them to know that these were hard decisions that were not made lightly, and I wanted to shake their hands and personally thank associates for their service and customers for their business."

"While we had to make difficult decisions, we also had ample opportunity to show that we were committed to taking care of our store associates. While other companies were cutting bonuses and eliminating 401(k) matches, we chose to continue those incentives for our associates, as well as annual pay increases. The Home Depot's founders, Bernie Marcus and Arthur Blank, said that if you take care of the associates, they will take care of the customers and everything else takes care of itself. I believe in that philosophy to my core . . . and our investment has paid off!"

Under Carol's leadership, the company achieved its revised financial targets a full year ahead of the goal, putting the company on a solid course toward a stellar financial condition, earning revenues of more than $70 billion and providing jobs for 331,000 people in 2012.

Knowing When to Walk Away

Never doubt the sheer power of core values consciously conceived. I first became fully aware of this power as recently as fifteen years ago. One of the women I most admire and who was a great mentor to me abruptly left her position as vice president of her company. All of us who knew her were deeply shocked. She was the company's first woman officer, and she was clearly on a track there to achieve a lot more. I was anxious to speak to her about her sudden departure, and, for her part, she was eager to explain.

She told me that she has always tried to live her life with integrity, and relied on her core values to guide the way she managed her life and career. Well, her bosses had asked her to cover up a company mistake. They asked her to lie to their customers and to their employees. When she responded that she could do no such thing, she was told that failing to get on board would "not be good for her career."

My friend was not intimidated. Not only did she refuse to "get on board" but also she told them that she would leave the company if they did not admit their mistake, take responsibility for it, and work toward making it right. When her bosses refused to do the right thing, she walked her talk. She left.

After this explanation, I was no longer shocked by her departure. Under the circumstances, I would have been shocked—and dismayed—had she *not* left. As for the company, it was successfully sued two years later for millions because an unreported flaw in a product had, tragically, led to a death. Bankruptcy followed.

By that time, of course, my friend and mentor had moved on to another firm, where she quickly achieved the same level of success she'd had with the former employer. Staying true to her values had given her the courage to make the decision to leave. Difficult? Yes. But it kept her on the path she herself had chosen long before her employer decided to leave it.

"If you can't harmonize your hopes, aspirations, and values within the context you're working in, then it's time you move away from that environment," says Rebecca Jacoby, the chief information officer and senior vice president of the IT and Cloud & Systems Management Technology Group at Cisco. Like my friend, Rebecca once had to walk away from a company due to a conflict in values concerning the company's handling of decisions about resources during a difficult economic time. "I had to decide how I would handle the situation, and it all circled back to understanding myself and the context of my environment, and being able to harmonize those two things. Ultimately I left the company."

It's worth noting that when you make tough decisions driven by core values, there's no guarantee that the world will immediately reward you for doing the right thing. That said, if you choose the path that allows you to live up to the standard of your own values, *again and again and again,* your chances of success start looking pretty great.

You Can't Have Everything—So Know What's Most Important

Of course we can't have it all. No one can. Life requires prioritizing and making difficult choices. But the secret to navigating those choices is a well-defined core of vision and values. If you know what's most important to you, you can make decisions with confidence and be satisfied with what you *did,* rather than mired in regret for what you *didn't.*

One of the most raw, honest conversations I've had on the subject of balancing family with work was with my colleague Penny Manuel, former executive vice president of engineering and construction services for Southern Company. Her husband, Don, left his own career so that he and Penny could relocate to pursue her professional dreams. In 2010 she took on one of the most challenging assignments of her career. She was responsible for managing major construction projects on seven sites, including the country's largest biomass facility in Nacogdoches, Texas, and twenty-first-century coal gasification in Kemper County, Mississippi. Eight months into the job, Don died very suddenly at age fifty-two.

"The first few months after his death," she says, "I was bitter and angry at myself for allowing work to interfere with what would be our last months together. It seemed to me that I had spent the last year of Don's life worried about the wrong thing."

Looking back, her perspective shifted. She told me she saw what she "couldn't see in real time," and offered this advice:

"Define the work-life balance for you, for your family, and for your career. Each of us makes choices every day. A professional career is hard and demanding, but it is what Don and I chose together, and he was proud of me. He allowed me to do what I do, and we both made sacrifices for it. Don't be afraid to work really hard. Don't be afraid to be bold. Don't be afraid to go somewhere you've never been. Believe in yourself, and don't be afraid."

Dare to set the target high, and reach it with courage and grace.

Dare to . . . Define Six Core Values

In the end, we each have to define our own core values. I have found that keeping my list and reviewing it often gives me the energy I need when confronted with tough decisions. Let me share the six that I've consciously defined to guide my vision and, in fact, my daily life.

- *Integrity.* I tell the truth and do what I say I will. If I can't do something I committed to, I tell those concerned why I cannot. I speak up when I see things that don't look right.
- *Growth.* I am committed to seeking continual personal development. There is so much to learn in the world, and I want to stay competitive.
- *Love.* I need love, and I have a lot to give: love of life, people, animals, and nature; most important, love of friends and family.
- *Giving.* True joy really does come from helping others. From those to whom much is given, much is expected. Whenever I can help someone, I do.
- *Fun.* Life is short. I need to enjoy the journey and not sweat the small stuff.
- *Faith.* I endeavor to be humble before the Lord and honor Him in all that I do.

    Your turn!

CHAPTER TWO

DARE TO KNOW YOURSELF

Develop Self-Assurance by Identifying Your Weaknesses

Know yourself. Don't accept your dog's admiration as conclusive evidence that you are wonderful.

ANN LANDERS

Successful executive leaders are self-aware. It's almost impossible to dare, and certainly impossible to lead, without knowing who you are. Clearly defining your vision and values on a regular basis is the first step toward that strong sense of self. But you also need to know where you fit in that vision, and that requires a clear and calm appraisal of your own strengths and weaknesses.

Susan Grant is the executive vice president of CNN News Services, a division of CNN Worldwide, and one of the strongest leaders I have ever met. Under Susan's stewardship, CNN Digital has become the Internet's leading news destination globally across various online and mobile platforms. And yet when I interviewed her for this book, Susan told me that the hardest, and best, thing she'd ever done was this: "to grasp the uncomfortable truth that, as a seasoned and successful business-sales-management executive, I still have far more to learn about myself."

The learning process began when Susan was faced with some critical feedback. She could have run from it, but her gut told her that it was right, and that she needed to make a change if she wanted better outcomes going forward. The feedback, so hard to hear at first, proved to be incredibly rewarding. "In the process of learning about myself, and taking charge of my *self*, I have found my gifts: I can clearly articulate my strengths, and I am purposeful about my life in ways I did not at first imagine," she says.

The Mentors Speak: On Knowing Yourself

Be true to yourself—a premise that starts with knowing who you are, what you want, and what you bring to the table. Go in with an approach that recognizes most people want to contribute and really try hard to do the right thing. If you can do this, you'll have an open mind and be able to solve problems and move things forward.

Rebecca Jacoby, *CIO and SVP, IT and Cloud & Systems Management Technology Group, Cisco*

Own and be proud of who you are and where you come from. If you are not, then go talk to a coach, therapist, priest, pastor, or rabbi. Do whatever it takes to know who you are and to own it.

Veronica Sheehan, *SVP, Global Network Operations and International IT, Turner Broadcasting System*

Surround yourself with a small network of people who will be honest with you—both positively honest and critically honest. I can build personal trust in a small network, and the feedback when I do something well helps overcome challenges.

Penny Manuel, *former executive VP of engineering and construction services, Southern Company*

My career has been full of personal challenges to my vision of my *self*, and, as I've progressed through life, I've come to see these challenges as choices: Do I choose to remain as or where I am, or do I choose to press forward?

Susan Grant, *executive VP, CNN News Services*

The best leaders know that there is always something to improve on. Perhaps you've heard the expression, "What got you here won't get you there." One of the chief reasons so many either get stuck in middle management or struggle once they make the leap to executive leadership is that the strengths that help managers thrive aren't uniformly the same as the strengths that help executives thrive. For example, deep domain expertise may have made you a star as you rose in your career. As an executive, that same domain expertise might inhibit your ability to delegate decision making, as I learned myself when I moved into technical fields as a CIO and found that certain gaps in knowledge were surprisingly an asset. As your career progresses, you can't rest on your accomplishments. You have to constantly assess what's needed to do the job and to what degree you're satisfying those requirements.

Those who accept that they have weaknesses and make a plan to improve them aren't just more capable, they're more confident—two of the most important ingredients when it comes to daring and leadership.

TO GET STRONG, ADMIT YOU'RE WEAK

One of my mentors, and one of the greatest female leaders I know, is Betty Siegel, who was formerly president of Kennesaw State University. She transformed that institution, located outside of Atlanta, from being a relative unknown to being the second-largest university in the state of Georgia. In fact, she was the first female president of any Georgia state university.

Betty has often said,

> The most important relationship you have is the one with yourself. You have to be feeling good about who you are when you look at yourself in the mirror *every*

morning. You need a clear vision of what you want to
achieve and an understanding of yourself. What you're
good at—and what you're not good at. This self-awareness and sense of what you want to achieve will make
you unstoppable. If you don't know yourself—and if
you don't ultimately feel good about the self you
know—you cannot know other people, and you certainly cannot lead others effectively.

One of the first things you do in the morning and one of
the last things you do at night is look in the mirror. The mirror
reflects your image, and that gives you a morning and evening
opportunity to accomplish a surprising amount of useful self-
analysis. Instead of looking in the mirror and focusing on what
you see on the outside, look beyond your physical attributes
and think about what's *inside.* What are your strengths—and
your weaknesses? Many of us are quick to see flaws in our
physical reflection, but less willing to explore the weaknesses
that we can't see, and that we think we can hide from others.

When you get to a place where you can calmly and honestly
evaluate yourself, owning up to areas you might improve instead
of ignoring them, you will find that you can act more confidently
and be more effective in your work. As your effectiveness
increases, so will your confidence. Likewise, as you feel more
confident, you will make more effective decisions. You've heard
of a *vicious* circle. Well, this is what is called a *virtuous* circle.

Peter Buckley, the dean of the School of Psychology at the
Medical College at Georgia Regents University, told me that
"the ability to improve your attitude and confidence is directly
tied to self-awareness. Having a clear vision of what you want,
knowing your strengths and weaknesses, and having the ability
to hear and be open to feedback are essential elements of a
confident attitude."[1]

The trouble is that most of us know much more about our
strengths than we do about our weaknesses. I taught a class

recently in which I asked students to think about their two greatest strengths. Most could identify them instantly. Then I asked them to identify their two biggest areas in need of development—their weaknesses. I promised I wouldn't ask them to share their weaknesses with the class, I just wanted them to raise their hand if they could immediately identify two weaknesses.

Not a single hand went up. They were stumped. They either couldn't think of two weaknesses or weren't willing to admit they had them.

I have consistently been amazed at the number of mid-career executives who have never been told about, and are not aware of, the things they need to work on. Even more astounding is the fact that they themselves have not been actively seeking input and feedback.

All of the women I interviewed for this book, women at the very top of their respective fields, were able to tell me about their weak areas. They knew what they were and could articulate how they were dealing with them. Many of them spoke about having team members to supplement their weaknesses. For instance, Veronica Sheehan, senior vice president of Global Network Operations and International IT for Turner Broadcasting System, told me, "My direct reports have a certain technical aptitude that I don't. I would be a poor example of a leader if I were too proud to capitalize on their strengths. Nobody has all the answers, and you cannot solve complex business problems alone."

The women I interviewed were also able to tell me about people they trusted who were on call to help coach them in dealing with their developmental challenges. These women don't take "negative" feedback personally. They embrace it.

Don't let some undiscovered, uninvestigated issue keep you from reaching the top rung on the corporate ladder. It's a cliché because it's a fact: we all have faults. You need to know your weaknesses and know them at least as intimately as you know your strengths. They can sabotage you and hold you back if you don't. Own your weaknesses so that you can conquer them—or, at the very least, learn to work around them.

Consider this: it is not awareness of our weak areas that erodes self-confidence, it is our fear of the unknown. Understand your personal assets as well as your liabilities, and you will be enabled to act with the assurance of self-knowledge.

DARE TO ASK FOR FEEDBACK

When you attempt to identify areas for improvement, first ask yourself what needs work. Start a list. When you run out of items on your own, start asking other people. This may make you feel vulnerable, but don't be afraid of criticism and analysis. They are gifts. Through critical self-examination and constructive criticism from others, you discover yourself more fully and deeply than ever before. By being proactive and asking for feedback, you open the door for others to give you input they might otherwise withhold.

I told the students in my class that to get started, they should ask their children, their spouse, or someone they trust. Our children can be quite candid. I can't tell you the number of times my daughter has told me I should stop wearing pantyhose because they are out of style. If you don't have children, a spouse or close friend can also be helpful. I have learned over time that it is only those who truly care for you who will be open and candid with their feedback, especially if the feedback is negative. That said, even those who care can be inclined to soft-pedal for fear of hurting your feelings.

Refuse to accept the proposition that you are a perfectly finished work of art. Nobody is, and nobody is even remotely complete. The urge to improve, not the comfortable conviction of self-satisfaction, drives success. When your children, your bosses, or your peers give you feedback about your weaknesses, listen and don't fight it.

I have a friend who told all her direct reports at their annual review that she was going to be brutally honest. After reviewing their strengths and accomplishments, she identified, for each direct report, one or two developmental areas of weakness with specific examples of how that weakness had made him or her

Do a 360

Upward assessments and 360-degree reviews are widely used in corporate America—and widely debated. A super comprehensive discussion of the 360-degree review concept was recently commissioned by the U.S. Office of Personnel Management. Entitled *360-Degree Assessment: An Overview*, it may be downloaded free of charge at www.opm.gov/perform/wppdf/360asess.pdf.

If you're interested in a formal assessment or 360-degree review, suggest it to your employer and offer some options, such as the Leadership Practices Inventory assessment (info at www.pfeiffer.com/WileyCDA/) or Birkman International (http://birkman.com), which offers both a well-regarded 298-question personality assessment and a 360-degree review process.

If you'd like to launch an independent 360-degree review, I recommend the 360 Assessment (www.360assessment.net/). It allows you to collect feedback anonymously from bosses, peers, employees, and customers—anyone, really—and delivers the results in a nicely formatted report. On your own, you can take a "light" version of the original Birkman assessment with the book *The Birkman Method*. The Gallup organization's online StrengthsFinder assessment is also available with the purchase of Gallup's eponymous book. Or consider conducting an informal 360-degree review. Reach out to a handful of friends and colleagues—peers, bosses, and direct reports—and ask them to give you some feedback on your most recent significant interaction with them. You can also ask them to help you identify habits that are negatively affecting your ability to do great work and move forward.

less effective in the past. Some of the individuals probed for more feedback as well as practical advice on how to change these weaknesses. Others came back with a long list of reasons why she was wrong or didn't understand the circumstances that caused them to perform as they did. These individuals took the feedback as a personal assault rather than the gift that it was. Those who tried to change were generally more successful in their roles going forward than those who fought the critique.

No one has made a better case for inviting high-quality, no-holds-barred feedback than Keith Ferrazzi in *Who's Got Your Back*: "In the end, the truth isn't going anyplace. Ignore it, and it will bite you in the bum," he writes. "Repress it, and it will almost always seep out or erupt in one way or another—usually at the worst time possible—resulting in mediocre long-term performance."[2]

Even when we disagree with feedback, we need to understand that others' perceptions of us are their reality, and if we don't understand and respond to what they perceive as weaknesses, their view of us will not change.

HOW I LEARNED TO STOP BUTTING IN

Count on it, it *is* possible to turn a weakness into a strength. All you need is planning, diligence, and a little help.

Early in my career I got feedback from several different sources, including someone I deeply trusted, that I was not a great listener. I accepted this information as the gift that it was, because I recognized that being a poor listener would certainly hinder my efforts to motivate my team to succeed. I acted on the information. I looked online for advice on productive listening, and I found some great ideas for developing better listening skills. I also asked my friends to help me understand why people thought I was a poor listener. Several told me that I

often "butted in" when people were trying to tell me something. Apparently, I was overly anxious to make my point of view
known before listening to their input first. This criticism rang
true with me. I knew—I know—I'm an extrovert, and this kind
of assertiveness is common among "our kind."

    I decided on a course of improvement. I consciously taught
myself to slow down and to curb my natural impulse to offer
solutions before allowing others to finish explaining their
position. This took a deliberate and vigilant effort, but it was
one that actually being aware of the problem enabled me to
make. Soon, I found that forcing myself to hear out the views of
others before I chimed in made me a much better decision
maker and leader. I was able to gather and digest more facts up
front. When my mouth was shut, my ears were open—and, with
them, my mind. Moreover, as people became accustomed to
my listening to them instead of cutting them off, they became
more open, more willing to share their insight and knowledge.

    People are more generous in expressing themselves to you
when they don't know whether their views and ideas are in
harmony or in conflict with yours. Seeking the views of others first
is essential if you want to avoid strangling input. This is especially
true if you are the leader of the team. When asked for my opinion,
I've learned to take a breath and remember that decision making
is always more about asking questions than making declarations.
So, instead of blurting out my take on an issue, I usually answer
with a question: "I'm not sure, what are *your* thoughts?"

    I did encounter one problem with forcing myself to hold off
on stating my opinion. I realized that my tendency to interrupt
was not due solely to overactive assertiveness. It was also the
product of my fear that if I did not immediately share my
thoughts, I would forget them. They would slip my mind. This is
a real possibility, of course. We have all experienced that
dreadful sensation of *I forgot what I was going to say.*

    To address this, I cultivated the habit of quickly jotting
down a few key words to mark my thoughts as I listened intently

---

Erase the Scoreboard

Don't let criticism or the awareness that you've made a mistake cripple you. In my experience, I've found that women find it harder to handle negative feedback than men do. Maybe it's because, growing up, boys tease and haze each other mercilessly. They compete, and they pick fights. They win or they lose, and then they move on. From an early age, boys become accustomed to battling, winning, losing, and still being friends after the fight is over. In contrast, many girls grow up being taught to "play nice" and seek approval, which makes them particularly uncomfortable when they are faced with a critique. We've grown up having learned to take criticism personally, and we don't forget about it easily. We've been taught to keep a mental scoreboard of the criticism we've received, and, grown up, we keep on keeping it. Why not dare to do a little erasing?

---

while others made their point. Only after they were finished did I express my opinion, referring to my jottings to ensure that I was leaving nothing out.

Holding my tongue and jotting down my passing thoughts turned out to be two very simple changes that allowed me to compensate for not being a naturally patient listener. These days, no one complains about my listening skills anymore, and because I get more candid opinions up front, I am able to be a better decision maker.

Rest assured, today there are other items on my list of things to work on. The process never ends.

GETTING THE BEST DATA

Asking others for feedback to guide you may be the very best way to help you identify biases and other counterproductive or even destructive habits of thought and behavior. Be careful to avoid relying exclusively on friends, who may be predisposed to "protect you" from what they perceive as painful. Seek and accept responses even from people you think don't like you. It is these people who will probably give you the most uncompromising criticism. It may be tough to take, but it is still a *gift*. You need to know what you don't know.

And there is a bonus. I've found that if you respond to criticism with "Thank you so much for telling me that," you can turn an adversary into a friend very quickly. Humility combined with gratitude—sincerely expressed—can defuse anger and make people more willing to share all sorts of valuable information with you.

Those of you who are already in a senior position have probably found it increasingly difficult to elicit frank and constructive feedback. Our common survival instincts make most of us naturally reluctant to criticize the boss, even when he or she *asks* for it. That means that at the top, you've got to be an expert at priming the pump to get feedback that's honest.

No matter from whom you solicit feedback—family, friends, or rivals—ask for a candid response, and make your request both sincere and believable. After most decisions I make and actions I take, I ask for candid feedback to determine what I can do better next time. People are generally reluctant to give you no-punches-pulled, constructive feedback unless they are certain that it is what you really want. Few of us enjoy hurting someone's feelings, so you must be perfectly sincere in your request for candor. Open the door to it, and people will tell you the truth.

Expect to be surprised by what you hear—and maybe unpleasantly so. Even if you think you've done something well, you should ask others specifically what could be improved. Incorporating what you learn from this blunt question will help you fine-tune your skills and be even better the next time you perform the same task. If you respond at all defensively when you do receive an unvarnished critique—if you betray irritation, offense, hurt feelings, or anger—you can bet it will be the last time that person, or anyone within earshot, will be candid with you.

As a leader, model the kind of constructive feedback you want for yourself by offering constructive feedback to others when needed. It is important to frame feedback so that the person on the receiving end understands that you have his or her best interest at heart. I have always found that it is most productive to begin conversations by talking about what is going well and the many assets an individual brings to the table. Positive comments create the open and supportive environment you need when the developmental discussion begins. If you can deliver feedback that inspires rather than deflates the person receiving it, you will encourage others become more constructively open with you. Be a helpful critic, and you will create a helpful critic.

SETTING A COURSE
FOR CHANGE

As important as it is to elicit and listen to feedback, don't let a single criticism send you heedlessly rushing to change your behavior, unless perhaps the advice comes from someone you really trust. Instead, listen and consider. Search for consistencies among the comments of more than one person. A good rule of thumb is that if you hear the same criticism from at least three people, you have probably discovered something you genuinely need to work on. If, however, one person tells you something that doesn't seem to fit with the issues others have raised, weigh that outlying, aberrant message carefully. Chances are it is not productive feedback for you.

Also realize that although criticism is valuable—indispensable, actually—there are some people who will criticize you not to help you and your enterprise improve, but actually to undermine your growth. Their motive may be envy or competition for recognition within the organization; it may be that they just don't want you to make changes that create more work for them. No matter. Don't waste too much time trying to guess. When someone attempts to undermine you, respond like an eagle does when she has to avoid chattering, shrieking crows: just fly higher. Don't let that person distract you.

Feedback from truly knowledgeable and selfless sources can help you shut out the negative comments aimed at nothing more than undermining your confidence. In addition to informally seeking feedback from those you trust, make use of whatever formal tools may be available. Most corporations conduct programs devoted to such topics as emotional intelligence and also provide personality assessments that will help you gain an objective understanding of yourself so that you can better understand others. Upward assessments, in which direct reports rate their boss, and 360-degree reviews, in which subordinates, bosses, and peers all review an employee, are prime examples. If you haven't used one of these tools, give it a try. Don't miss any opportunity to gain knowledge about yourself and how to work better with others. Remember, the very best leaders know what their weaknesses are, and they work *every single day* to close the gap between aspiration and performance.

Once you've decided what you're committed to working on, do your homework. You will discover that people have more weaknesses in common than strengths, so you will be able to find a wealth of information on virtually any deficiency by talking with others. Pick the brains of friends and colleagues. Reach out to people you admire and trust. If you've got a bad habit, ask them to alert you when they see this behavior surface. If you feel embarrassed about asking friends to help you, the Web is a great place to find information on any developmental need you have, and there are a number of places where you can find mentoring online. If you can be more aware of counter-productive or downright destructive habits, you can do much to suppress, eliminate, or transform them.

BACK TO THE MIRROR

To rise in your career, and especially to make that all-important transition from middle management to senior management, you need a well-defined vision and a thorough understanding of your strong points as well as the areas that require development. Do you know where you need to improve and what you're great at? Are you tapping into everyone who can help you grow and lead?

Looking at yourself in the mirror should neither send you into a tailspin nor soothe you into mindless self-congratulation. It should push you to strive to be the leader who identifies and actively works on personal developmental needs, the leader who has open dialogue with her team. The strongest leaders are those who are aware of themselves as well as everyone around them. They know what they want and how to go about getting it. Dare to know yourself, and join them.

Dare to . . . Accept Feedback Graciously

How well you receive feedback often determines whether people feel safe being honest and open with you. Prepare yourself with this checklist.

✓ Listen calmly and monitor your body language.
✓ If you feel defensive, take a deep breath. Remember, this is just one point of view.
✓ Thank the speaker and let him or her know you'll take time to think about what he or she has told you.
✓ Follow up in a positive manner. If you decide to take actions based on the feedback, let the person know.

CHAPTER THREE

———————————

DARE TO STAND OUT

Differentiate Yourself and Become Your Own Best Advocate

Personal branding is the ultimate investment in yourself. If you don't, why should you expect anyone else to?

RACHEL QUILTY, AUTHOR OF *BRAND YOURSELF*

Y ou must dare to stand out to get noticed. Only by being noticed will you rise to lead.

I learned this lesson the hard way when I was pretty fresh out of college, working in a middle-management role in a big corporation. I had heard about an opening in another department and, intrigued, looked into it. As soon as I did, I realized I *really* wanted the job. So I approached my boss. He listened, and he not only gave me his blessing but also volunteered to go to the hiring manager, let him know about my interest, and tell him what an asset I had been to his department.

It seemed to me that I was golden. Seeking nothing more than encouragement, I came away with a full-on advocate—someone to apply for the job on my behalf. What luck!

But as time went by, I heard nothing more about the job, until I discovered that it had been filled by someone else. I swallowed my disappointment and went on with my work until, sometime later, I bumped into the hiring manager.

41

I asked him if he had any feedback for me on why *I* had not been considered.

"You never applied!" the man said, his eyes wide with surprise.

"But my boss . . ."

"Never spoke to *me*. Sorry."

In an agony of frustration, I called my dad, but quickly learned I'd gone to the wrong source for sympathy.

"If you wanted that job, you should have gone directly to the hiring manager and told him," he said to me.

Instantly, I realized that although I'd lost an opportunity, I had gained a valuable lesson. If I wanted to go far in my career, I couldn't afford to rely on someone else to be the secondhand messenger of my ambitions. I had to take control and let people know who I was and what I wanted.

This lesson is important for *anyone* with the desire to enter into senior leadership, but it's particularly urgent for women focused on those top roles. We still face unique challenges compared to men when it comes to being recognized and celebrated as leaders. Now, there are many sobering studies about workplace behaviors that enhance the stature of men and diminish that of women, and even more strategies for how women can compensate for those differences. Just for the moment, rather than having you chase studies and suffer over how to manage the details of the gender dilemma, I want you to do something much more empowering: I want you to dare to stand out on your own terms. Here we'll discuss how to cultivate an unassailable personal brand around integrity, excellence, and results, and how to become a gracious yet relentless advocate for yourself in the workplace.

Do those two things well, and I guarantee that their combined effect will take you further than the vagaries of workplace bias will ever hold you back.

UNDER THE MICROSCOPE

Build a great personal brand, and success will follow. Simply put, your personal brand is the way you present yourself. It represents the value proposition you offer your colleagues, subordinates, bosses, customers, and community. It proclaims to the world how you stand out—and simultaneously fit in.

Competition for the top jobs in corporate America is tough. There are far more qualified candidates than job openings. That means it's up to you to make sure your brand is one that helps you stand out from the crowd. People make assumptions about you and even decide whether to do business with you before ever meeting you, on the basis of your personal brand.

Realize that you have a brand whether you've consciously crafted one or not. Once you enter into a leadership position at any level, you will find that you are communicating even when you think you have nothing in particular to say. The more responsibility you acquire, the more closely the lens of your company's collective microscope will focus on you. You have to be better than the norm. People will watch what you *do* even more than they monitor what you say. Actions, as the old saying goes, really do speak louder than words.

And I'm not just talking about the big things, the big decisions. Your employees and other staff will watch when you walk into the building in the morning. They will look to see if you smile and say hello—or if you scowl and growl. They will observe how you interact with people at all levels and how you respond to challenges both great and trivial.

Does being this closely watched make you uneasy? Well, the good news is that you *are* being watched. This means you are indeed standing out. So, it's your time to shine. Perform well, and the close scrutiny becomes a marvelous opportunity. Perform poorly, and it becomes a daily liability. Choose, therefore, to perform well.

DISTINGUISH YOURSELF WITH INTEGRITY

Like product brands, personal brands come in many varieties and promise different things. But I would argue that all truly successful personal brands have integrity as their central promise. A career, like every other aspect of business, is built on positive relationships. These relationships, in turn, are founded on trust. Whom are we willing to trust? People who embody and broadcast integrity, which means that they'll tell the truth, do the right thing, and not withhold important information.

Years ago, people could agree on some of the most important things with a simple handshake. Anything folks "shook on" was sealed with their word, which meant that both parties had staked their reputation on performing honorably, on absolutely and meticulously following through.

Even the most traditional among us are a little more circumspect these days and take care to supplement a handshake and word of honor with legally binding contracts, guarantees, and receipts. The symbolism may be different, but the bottom line remains the same: your integrity and transparency are the most important assets you have, the core components of your personal brand, the values because of which you most want to stand out and fit in.

The 2013 Edelman Trust Barometer suggests that trust in business leadership remains dismally low, although it is finally on the rise.[1] Of the more than twenty-six thousand general population respondents surveyed, only 19 percent said they trusted business leaders to make ethical and moral decisions. In other words, 81 percent of people don't trust that executives will do the right thing. Only 18 percent said they trusted leaders to "tell them the truth" regardless of how complicated and unpopular it might be.

You would think that creating trust would be the bare minimum essential to business. Going by the stats, however, if you manage to make yourself the "integrity brand," you will stand out on that differentiator alone.

Trust is the essence of integrity, a core trait that must be guarded with the most exacting fortitude. Compromising integrity is like breaking an egg. There's no making it whole again. In the end, it really doesn't matter what else you have if you have no integrity. It doesn't matter how smart or attractive you are. It doesn't matter what you achieved in the past if people think they cannot trust you now. Tarnish your brand by giving others a reason to stop trusting you, and you cannot be successful. If your colleagues, customers, and vendors don't trust you, they won't stick with you when you need them most—if they even do any business with you. Those who do not follow the rules can end up in jail. Over the past two or three decades, the handcuffed CEO "perp walk" has become a televised icon of corporate malfeasance.

Without integrity, nothing else about you has meaning. Make this the core of your personal code of ethics and the foundation of your personal brand. The beauty of integrity as a foundation is that there is virtually no limit to how high you can build on it.

Business is a risky endeavor, but there's one thing I can promise your career will deliver: moments of extreme challenge that put your integrity to the test. In Chapter One, I talked about the need to develop core values. Acting with integrity means acting in accordance with your values. Rather than wait for a challenge, take time *right now* to think through what you consider acceptable, right, and valuable in your work and your life. Don't accept uncritically the ideas and values a coworker or a boss hands you. Examine them, and use them to help you decide on *your* standards. Articulate and define these standards for your-self. Incorporate the best and the most productive into your brand—the promise of the value you offer. The standards that you choose will be the structure that supports how you conduct your life both in and outside of business.

AVERAGE IS OVER

If you are really determined to dare to stand out, decide to be a star. Stars stand out. They are warm and brilliant. They illuminate paths that others follow. You have the potential to be a star, lighting the way for your colleagues as well as for younger women who will follow the path you've brightened.

You're going to need to shine bright, because "average is over," as Thomas Friedman declared.[2] Those who are just average are likely to find their job outsourced or to be replaced by a computer. Never has it been more important to cultivate a brand of excellence. Hala Moddelmog, president of Arby's, says: "There is no substitute for being prepared, practiced, and knowledgeable. Do your homework, gather the data to educate yourself on the topic, and share your point of view. Most important, get the results! In the end, results are what you are hired to produce, and corporate success does not come to anyone without producing those results."

I can't stress enough the importance of being known as someone who gets results, if you want to climb up the corporate ladder. If you can build a reputation for delivering *results with integrity*, you can overcome almost any Achilles' heel. Rebecca Jacoby from Cisco told me, "[By getting results] you become associated with success and build a track record. Everyone has strengths and weaknesses, but your track record is what allows people to notice your strengths and forgive your weaknesses."

Lora G. Weiss, lab chief scientist and the technical director of autonomous systems at Georgia Tech Research Institute, stressed the need for women in technical fields not just to reach for excellence but in fact to outdo their male colleagues. "Female engineers' grades out of school need to be better than those of their male counterparts," she says, "if they want to avoid the accusation and misconception that they were hired just because they are girls. The higher expectation may seem unfair, but . . . keeping this in mind can go a long way— throughout your career, in fact. We live in a numbers world. Everyone is assessed by metrics of some sort. If your numbers are better than his are, then you must be better."

I once had to work double-time building my personal brand to convince my male colleagues that I was qualified to lead. I had just been hired to re-enter a department I had worked in long before as an underling. Now I would be its leader, the boss of men who had once trained me. Before I arrived on the scene, my boss, whom I'll call Fred, sat down with the team I would be leading. Naturally, they were anxious to find out whether their new boss had been hired from within their group. Fred sat them down and made the following announce- ment: "We had many great candidates from the team, but because of our affirmative action goals, we're bringing in a woman, Becky Blalock." In other words, he told the entire group that I was hired not because I was uniquely capable, but rather because I was a woman and they needed to appease affirmative action.

I only found out because the handful of women who were in the room for the announcement passed the story on to me. When I called Fred, he apologized and said he thought that blaming it on affirmative action was the best way to cool the egos of all the men in the room who had been passed over for the job. I was apoplectic. He had completely undermined me. But rather than make a fuss up the chain or demand that he gather everyone together again to publicly recant, I took matters into my own hands and embarked on a one-woman rebranding campaign.

I took every single employee, starting with the guys, out for a one-on-one lunch. It allowed me to show them who I was face- to-face, and to start to build a relationship. Then, I operated day to day as I always had—with measured integrity and transparency, constantly asking for feedback, doing everything I could to make sure our team delivered results and shared in the victories.

Over time my team and I built a track record of big wins, and Fred's idiotic remark was completely forgotten. But if I hadn't spent the time and effort up front to rebuild my brand with the group, we might not have been so successful.

CREATE OPPORTUNITIES TO RADIATE EXCELLENCE

Becoming a star is about acting with initiative and excellence in whatever role you play. It's about coming in every day and being the very best you can be. It is about consciously thinking about and designing the image you want to project. It's about doing your current job well and not being constantly focused on the next one.

"I started out as a file clerk, but I was the best darn file clerk I could be, and soon my work ethic paid off," Lyn McDermid told me. "I moved up to secretary. It was my boss, an executive in the shipyard, who suggested I apply for the Newport News Shipbuilding and Dry Dock Company Apprentice Program." She was the very first woman to join the program, and the success and confidence she created there kicked off a career that eventually took her to the role of chief information officer for the Federal Reserve System in 2012, after many years holding the same position at a $15 billion power and energy company headquartered in Richmond, Virginia.

Initiative is action. Don't sit and wait for someone to tell you what needs to be done to overdeliver in your position. I can't tell you how many people in middle management I've watched make this mistake, and so there they stayed. Determine these needs for yourself. Satisfy them with action. Figure out what has to be done and start doing it. You've got to be smart enough to determine what your team, your customers, and your company need, even if they don't know it themselves. This may not be exactly in your job description, but this is, in fact, the unwritten reality of every job of any importance—the higher up the ladder the go, the fewer directions you will get from others.

Identify projects in your company that provide the foundation of knowledge and experience you need for the long term. In most corporations, these are pretty easy to spot. They're tough, they're mundane, or they're both. If you see a job that needs doing or an opportunity that you want, take it. Then make it work for you.

Early in my own career, I saw that nobody wanted to do the budget for our department. Little wonder. It was grunt work, but something that was vital to how we operated our business. I understood that, which is precisely why I said, "I'll take it." Nobody raised a protest, of course, because nobody else wanted it, but it was undoubtedly one of the best learning experiences I had.

I learned about the budgeting system itself and how costs get allocated. I learned how there is an awful lot of wiggle room inside any complex budget. I learned how people game the system. Years later, as CIO of a major corporation, I managed a $450 million budget, which was a significant part of my job. Being able to draw from my early hands-on experience in learning how expenses get booked and things get reported was extremely helpful. Not many little girls dream about doing budgets when they grow up, but I am grateful that I owned that task at the start of my career. Leadership is built on a foundation of just such "grunt" assignments.

Be constantly on the lookout for special opportunities to demonstrate a broader range of skills and abilities, even if it means taking on projects that no one else wants to touch. Lyn told me a similar story about how she made the leap to the executive suite by jumping into "a huge, risky project that needed help." In a difficult time, she focused on the success of the project and everyone associated with it, including the project leader. "My contribution was recognized, and I was promoted to an executive position soon after," she says.

Later in my career, when I wanted to shift out of finance into business development, I faced a new branding challenge: I had great interpersonal skills, but in my role at the time, I hadn't had any opportunity to prove it—*to shine.* And so I kept getting passed over for those jobs. People in middle management face this challenge all the time. "In assessing candidates for senior executive roles, business organizations look to the ranks of middle managers for evidence of the leadership skills capable of mobilizing and inspiring," explained Molly Burke, former general counsel for GE Energy Services, when telling me of her own struggle. "Middle managers are functional leaders, who often have a difficult time demonstrating these skills because their role is often perceived to be to support the organization's objectives from a functional point of view rather than to formulate strategy and lead the execution."

Molly knew she had to find an opportunity to demonstrate leadership beyond what her role afforded. Opportunity struck when she was asked to relaunch a hub of GE's Women's Network in Atlanta. The local hub had withered under the challenge of mobilizing a thousand or so women across more than thirty business locations throughout the metropolitan area. Molly took on the project, determined to reinvigorate the local network by convincing male and female leaders across the business to participate in a series of live programs in the Atlanta region.

By the end of the first year, her strategy had attracted a robust and engaged membership, which had centrally planned events as well as smaller gatherings at the individual business sites. "Our hub was soon recognized as a leader, and I was chosen to host the GE-wide, invitation-only women's conference in Atlanta the following year," says Molly. That conference would put her leadership in direct view of the chairman and all the senior business leaders in the company. Says Molly, "While I could have said that I had more than enough to do with my job and my kids, this experience enabled me to demonstrate my leadership to a wider audience and secured my promotion."

The Mentors Speak: On Standing Out

Working in Asia, Europe, and the Middle East for my start-up software company as a twenty-six-year-old was one of my biggest career challenges. I knew at the time that I had a great handle on my product and the opportunity for the major corporations that were interested in our technology, but I had no experience doing deals. I jumped in with both feet. The first thing I did was call around and identify people who could help. Then I created a personal board of directors to help me navigate the waters by region and country. I found highly experienced people who helped me understand what I should expect, how I should dress, how to carry myself, and how to manage my customers both personally and professionally.

Genevieve Bos, CEO, IdeaString

You have to start somewhere, and standing on the sidelines and shutting down after the first "no" is not going to get you ahead. Don't give up. Just keep moving forward.

Tena Clark, CEO and chief creative officer,
DMI Music and Media Solutions

My breakthrough opportunity came when the organization I was working for merged with another. The merger brought about tremendous change, and with change always comes opportunity. In the midst of this, I expressed myself boldly in meeting with top executives to voice my commitment to the organization and interest in growing professionally.

Martha McGill, COO, Miami Children's Hospital

Follow these steps: know yourself, know how you're perceived, know your audience, think about how you want to be perceived. Connect those dots to make the most of yourself and your opportunities.

Kat Cole, president, Cinnabon

SWEATING THE SMALL STUFF

Building a brand on integrity, excellence, and results is valuable and challenging in itself. But you can't stop there. Don't make the mistake of getting the "big stuff" right, but then failing to have it be noticed because the devil is in the details. Remember, your brand isn't just made up of those crucible moments when you're called to take a stand. It's also communicated in small, everyday gestures and in "superficial" choices, such as what you wear into the office each day.

It is important to review your own behavior continuously and strive to keep improving it. Be aware of yourself; of how you appear to others; and of how you interact with everyone, even—no, *especially*—people at the end of the chain of command. After all, there are more of them.

Integrity Requires Reliability

You may have heard the saying, "It takes a thousand good acts to create trust, and one bad act to break it." Fortunately, breaking trust is easy to avoid by rigorously observing a single rule: *if you say you're going to do something, do it.*

When asked if they are trustworthy, few people will say no. Nevertheless, many fail to demonstrate trustworthiness in the so-called "little things," particularly as they rise in influence and stature in their organization. The quality of reliability may not seem high minded, but it is a practical component of trust. Obviously, failing to deliver a job on time is a major lapse in living up to your commitment, but even failing to make a phone call you promised to make can be damaging.

"Is she reliable?" a corner-office type asks your colleague about you.

As your colleague starts to reply, all that comes to mind is that you still owe him a phone call. How will he answer?

Also, make it your invariable habit to appear on time. There is no "fashionably" late in business. No matter how good your excuse for making ten others around a conference table wait for your tardy arrival, all they'll ultimately remember is that you weren't there. Being on time is both the fulfillment of a promise and proof that you respect the time of others and that you follow through on your commitments, whether big or small.

Following through on your word builds trust. Failure to follow through erodes your reputation. There are always legitimate reasons why you can't do something. At the very least, call to say you can't make it. If you're going to miss a deadline, big or small, let people know. Apologize, even if the reason you can't follow through is totally out of your control. People can be very forgiving, but if you fail to demonstrate trustworthiness when it comes to the small things, they will be reluctant to trust you on the big ones. You build your brand of trustworthiness through dependability, promptness in responding, and faithfulness in follow-through—on absolutely everything.

You Need to Look the Part

Senior business leaders become so accustomed to serving others—peers, employees, bosses, investors, clients, and customers—that frequently they neglect themselves. This applies especially to women, who, along with juggling the pressures of their career, also tend to spend significantly more time on housework and parenting duties than their partner (in the case of a married mother and father).[3] They are often so busy taking care of everyone else that it becomes easy to neglect their own health and welfare as they pursue their professional goals. This tendency not only is physically and mentally destructive but also can destroy a career. If you are not at your best, you cannot deliver your best. It's vitally important that you take care of yourself by prioritizing sleep, exercise, and anything you need to do to stay mentally and physically healthy.

Taking care of yourself is most important—but letting *others* know you take care of yourself is almost as crucial. There is undeniably a visual component to your personal brand, and although it may be considerably less important than your integrity or your track record, you wear it much more on your sleeve. People don't know whether you're as good as your word when they meet you, but they're already making judgments about that and a million other things based simply on what they *see*. For both men and women, attractiveness matters. Fortunately, it's less about being "pretty" and more about how you style and carry yourself.

One of my mentors, Amanda Brown-Olmstead, the founder of a public relations and event planning firm, is always dressed to the hilt and carries herself with confidence. Highly successful in business, she conducts herself professionally at all times.

Early in our friendship, I said to her, "You are the epitome of grace and charm." Her reply has stuck with me for years: "I have to be. I'm self-employed. The way I dress and carry myself says how seriously I take myself. If I don't dress professionally and act professionally, my prospects and clients think, 'She's not going to take my business seriously.' When I'm trying to sell my services, I want people to think that everything about me says I'm going to take care of their business and do it well."

Dressing thoughtfully and carrying yourself with impeccable professionalism are not symptoms of vanity. They are all about your brand, which, in turn, is about what you will do for others. A brand is not value. It is a promise to deliver value.

When I entered the workforce, we women thought we had to act and dress more like men to be successful. We wore closed-toe shoes and little bow ties around our shirt collars, and we never, ever wore anything that showed cleavage.

What a difference thirty-plus years make! Today, we businesswomen dress in suits or dresses that flatter our figure rather than conceal it. The only taboo is wearing anything that sends a message that we're not serious about business. You've heard the phrase, "You don't get a second chance to make a first impression." Research indicates that people really do form an initial impression of someone within the first three to six seconds of contact. Make sure that the one they form about *you* is favorable. Ensure that what you wear and how you're groomed communicate your brand as powerfully as possible. This means you should dress *now* for your *next* job, your next role, your next promotion.

It may go without saying, but the rules for dressing as an influential leader are different from what might have worked earlier in your career. Consider a 2005 study, replicated by another set of researchers in 2009, that found that a woman in a low-status job could dress "sexy" without it affecting people's assessment of her intelligence or capabilities. Not so for women in high-status jobs, in which dressing provocatively rather than professionally leads to strikes against both.[4] In other words, a short skirt and cleavage might not count against you when you're an administrative assistant, but they make you look unprofessional when you're the boss.

Your Smile Has Power

Executives are often so preoccupied that they are hardly aware of the employees around them. Early in my career as a supervisor, I was fortunate that an employee told me I looked so serious that it was downright intimidating for my staff to be around me. I was shocked. Not only did I thank the employee for his comment but also, from that moment on, I made it a point to look everyone in the eye and say hello. I understood that, as the leader of an organization, I set the tone for the team. Did I want a tone of fear and intimidation? Of course not. I wanted to create a pleasant and more productive workplace for my team members, and so I worked hard to change my demeanor to produce the tone I wanted.

I realized that I was facing what was essentially a communication problem. Unbeknownst to me, my body was delivering the wrong message. Fortunately, in contrast to many other problems in communication, which are often complex and subtle, this one was remarkably easy to solve. All I had to do was smile and be the first one to reach out my hand. As the leader, you are the one who should take the initiative to reach out and make others feel welcomed and comfortable.

Smiles are so simple, and they are absolutely free. Moreover, a smile is like a yawn; it is incredibly contagious. A simple, unsubtle smile is the most powerful signal you can send that you are approachable. Smile, and you create a magnetic field. People will gravitate to you, curious to discover what makes you so happy.

You want people to remember you in a positive way, as a listening leader who walks the talk and shares a smile. I'm not saying it's always easy, but if you continue to try, in time it will become a habit. Your smile and your good listening skills will be part of your brand, something that will separate you from the rest of the pack.

TOOT YOUR HORN

Many of us women are daunted by the very thought of promoting the great work we do. Some of us attribute our success to other people—or, even worse, to good fortune. As in so many other aspects of our behavior, biology and culture conspire to keep us from sounding the occasional fanfare. Women are taught from very early on, and perhaps are physiologically hardwired, to focus on collaborating and fitting in, whereas men are encouraged to compete. For men, winning takes precedence over collaboration, and standing out (and above) seems to them far more imperative than fitting in. Nobody likes a blowhard, but most of us walk around with the nagging sense that it is far less attractive for a woman to promote herself than it is for a man to do the same.

Too bad. You are in business, and it is a big part of your business to get the word out so that you can stand out. Never assume that your accomplishments "speak for themselves," that people are somehow naturally and inevitably aware of your great work. If you decide to wait for others to toot the horn for you, you are probably in for a long wait—maybe an interminable one.

The good news is that you don't have to focus exclusively on yourself. In fact, I have found that the best way to broadcast my value is to broadcast the great work of my team. I made it a practice to write a note to my boss to brag—yes, *brag*—whenever one of my team members did something wonderful. Very often, my note would prompt him to call the individual in question to deliver his or her personal thanks for a great job. This, of course, would make individual employees feel tremendously appreciated, and it would also let them know that I, their supervisor, credited them. Everyone benefitted. Employees looked great and felt great. I looked good. And the boss was happy.

If you want to be the person who rises in your company, brag about your team, daily if possible—whenever something good happens on your watch. You are always safe if you're bragging about your team's achievements, not your own—and yet doing so schools your boss on just how effective a leader you are. Moreover, if you want great work to be repeated, acknowledge it when it is produced. Most recognition is free, but it can accomplish tremendous things, motivating those around you to excel, lifting morale, and driving success. Just about everyone responds positively to genuine praise, and that can help you attract the best talent. All employees want to work with a leader who appreciates their efforts and helps them be more successful.

In most corporations, there is a political process that determines where the company will invest its internal dollars. It's called budget time. Your objective, as a leader, is to ensure that others are keenly aware of the value your team adds to the enterprise. Stating concrete goals and publically celebrating their attainment lets those in charge of budgets know where to invest the money. You need to clearly and effectively articulate your team's accomplishments to seek recognition for them. I never hesitated to apply for awards for our work, and I made it a habit to nominate people on my team for public recognition through *individual* awards.

Know what? Most of the time, we would win.

Make no mistake: to win, of course, your team has to be doing work worthy of recognition. But you'll find that if you make winning, and the recognition and other rewards that go with it, a priority, your team will start producing work at a high level—a level that's *worth* recognition.

Winning awards not only trumpets your value within your company but also broadcasts to competitors, to the public, to shareholders, to potential customers, and to others that yours is a world-class organization. The best companies with the most prominent brands understand how powerful a message this is. That is why companies are never shy about including their awards in their advertisements—frequently building entire commercials around them.

Some of the best advertising is free. The media can increase the volume and range of your horn. Reporters are workers who perpetually have a problem to solve: they need news. They are always on the lookout for someone to quote or who can help them with real-world research. Become a reliable source, and you will find numerous media outlets through which you can promote the work of your team under the brand of your own name.

ASK FOR MORE

People seem to treat the pay gap between men and women like they do the weather: they think it's something to talk about but not something they can actually change. There is at least one thing every woman can do to improve her pay, and that's to master the art of negotiation. Asking for more money is the height of self-advocacy, and apparently the most difficult form of it for many women.

In their book *Women Don't Ask: Negotiation and the Gender Divide*, authors Linda Babcock and Susan Laschever successfully make the case that women are sacrificing hundreds of thousands of dollars of pay over the course of their career by failing to negotiate, starting from their first job; by having lower salary expectations (between 3 and 32 percent lower) than those of men; and by failing to practice the skills that make for effective haggling. When Babcock asked women to describe the experience of negotiating, they used words like "scary" and "like going to the dentist." Men said "fun," "exciting," and "like winning a ball game."[5]

What's going on? In part, we women have been taught from our childhood that it is rude to ask for money. And again, we are socialized to be team players, collaborative, and not self-serving. These patterns of behavior are so ingrained in us that they are difficult for us to recognize. It wasn't until I rose to a senior position and managed both men and women that I saw and understood the stark differences. Men were bold about asking for more money. It really shocked me because *I* never did this in my career, and the women I managed never came to me to ask for more money, either. I had been active in seeking new opportunities, but I was always so grateful for my job that it never occurred to me to negotiate for a higher salary. My guess it that this is typical for most women.

The bottom line is this: getting a raise is ridiculously simple. You won't get it if you don't ask for it. It is perfectly appropriate for you to ask for a raise or to negotiate your starting salary upward when you've earned it. Always negotiate for higher compensation. Nobody does it for you.

In recent years, I'm proud to say, I have been much more aggressive in this area. I was approached not long ago by a company that wanted me to consult for them on an hourly basis. I let them know I would not work on an hourly basis. If they wanted me, they would need to pay me a retainer. I asked several people I know who do similar consulting about their arrangements. They told me how much they were being paid, and I set my retainer accordingly. Then I made my case to the prospective employer as to why I was worth it. They balked, but then came back with what I had requested. I was happy, and they had more respect for me and were more inclined to trust my work because I was not willing to accept less.

When you're asking for a pay raise, consider these suggestions:

- *Get the timing right.* Don't ask for a raise when the company is laying people off or if the earnings just released were significantly down. The very best time to ask is when you have just received some public recognition.
- *Set the meeting.* Ask your boss for a face-to-face meeting to have a discussion about your career. You'll have a better conversation in person, and it's harder for your boss to turn you down when he or she is looking you in the eye.
- *Get the facts.* Go to Salary.com or another trusted statistical source to obtain objective data on what other employers are paying for your job. If possible, talk to coworkers and see what they are making—although you should scrupulously

respect any stated rules your company may have in place on the subject of disclosing salaries.

- *Show **them** the money.* Use data to show how your performance has contributed to the company's bottom line. Also clarify how your job has changed or evolved since your salary was last set. Have you taken on new responsibilities or added to your workload?
- *Formulate the amount you need to close the gap.* Remember, there are forms of compensation to consider in addition to salary, including more time off, paid educational opportunities, or retirement benefits.
- *Show your potential.* Having made your case, be prepared to articulate how you'll continue to grow your responsibility in the organization.
- *If denied, regroup.* Ask for specific feedback on why. Make the request positive, and don't take the feedback personally, respond to it defensively, or start an argument. If you allow rejection to ruin your attitude, your boss will believe he or she made the right decision.

SPEAK UP, *PLEASE*

One of the most powerful ways to build your brand, and that of your organization, is to develop strong presentation and public speaking skills. As a leader, you may need to be the spokesperson for your team or organization. I sought and accepted as many speaking engagements and opportunities to spend time with key audiences as I could. I actively looked for ways to promote the accomplishments of my team and our company.

I am sometimes asked if I can define a pivotal time or event that I feel is responsible for helping to launch my career. Although I believe it was a series of many little successes, I do often jump to one particular event.

My boss had selected me to make a presentation in front of the CEO and all the top company leadership about the success and added revenue that a new program I was leading had generated. I prepared for days for this presentation and had state-of-the-art visuals to support me. I was scared to death but practiced how to move and use the space. I decided I would not stand behind the podium; I would walk around the room and engage the executives present by asking them questions. It came together very well, and I received excellent feedback on my delivery and was awarded additional funding for the program. More important, the next month I was notified of my selection to be part of the high-potential program in our company. I am convinced that my strong performance "on stage" for this presentation is what helped me stand out and get noticed. I encourage you to leverage this type of opportunity if you are fortunate enough to have one come your way—and if one doesn't, seek it out!

You may have heard Jerry Seinfeld's bit about public speaking. He says that studies show that the majority of people rank public speaking just *above* death as their greatest fear. In other words, most of us would rather be lying in the casket than standing beside it giving the eulogy! It's more funny than it is factual, but it doesn't feel far from the truth. If you are intimidated by the prospect of making a speech, you are hardly alone. The upside is that when you rise to speak, you can do so with the knowledge that nearly every person in your audience would rather it be you than them on the podium. They want *you* to succeed. They want to enjoy *your* talk, and they want to learn something from it. And they are already grateful to you because *you* are talking, which means *they* don't have to. In short, they are most likely to be an inherently friendly audience.

Very few people are naturally good at delivering a public message, but if you are going to be a successful leader, you must learn to make powerful presentations. This isn't just about the words you communicate. Even the most exciting message can be lost if delivered with a voice that displays no emotion or feeling. Your responsibility as a speaker, especially when you're just starting out, is to spend just about as much time working on your delivery and visual impact as you do on the speech itself. I recommend recording yourself doing a practice run and watching it at least twice through—once without sound, to focus on what the audience would be seeing, and once just listening to the tone of your voice.

Effective public speakers, like effective leaders, focus not only on their voice and their physical presence but also on what their audience wants and needs to hear. This does not mean you should pander by sacrificing your message, your ideas, or your values in an effort to deliver something "palatable." Your responsibility as a speaker is first and foremost to speak the truth (which may or may not be pleasant to hear). To be a truly effective speaker, however, you should ensure that the truth you deliver concerns issues that are of genuine value and great interest to your listeners.

One of the most effective ways to connect with your audience is to ask them questions. Given the opportunity to address an audience, we all naturally assume that our job is to tell them things they don't already know. There is nothing wrong with this view, unless you allow it to cancel out another aspect of your job as a communicator. It is not just to tell, but also to ask.

If you set yourself up exclusively as a teller, members of your audience will define themselves strictly as receivers. They will see your role as active, theirs as passive—and a lot of people are very good at passivity. Many are so good, in fact, that they will drift off into lower consciousness, semiconsciousness, or even unconsciousness. I find that asking questions really keeps the audience engaged.

Finally, here is the ultimate weapon in the war for an audience's mind. Perhaps you have encountered the acronym WIIFM, which stands for "What's in it for me?" There is no more powerful way to connect with an audience or a team than by answering this question for them. We all want to hear information that will help us do our jobs better or make our lives easier and more successful. No wonder writer and speech expert Steve Brown says his first principle of communication is to remember this: "Generally, people are more interested in themselves than they are in you."[6]

When you address any group in business, including your own working group, tailor your choice of topic and your choice of language to them. Make it your goal to be a translator—to render your goals, purposes, and ideas in terms that have meaning for them. Use your material to develop different messages for different audiences, different teams tackling different issues, different people in need of different information. For example, when you speak to members of the company's board, talk to them about risk, forecasting, and market position. If your audience is the CEO, bring up innovation, competitive position, and debt. If you're talking to the legal team, talk about mergers and acquisitions, contract law, intellectual property, and force majeure. The CMO wants to hear about the competition, brand impact, market share, and new ways to attract customers; the CFO, budgets and cost-saving ideas; and the COO, operations availability. When talking to your own team members, realize that they want to know how well the company is performing and what its challenges are. They also want to know what they can personally do to help the company be more successful.

One day, a young woman I mentor asked me to sit in on a meeting so that I could give her feedback on her presentation style. She and several other high-potential employees were speaking to an executive group. She did a wonderful job in her delivery and in providing context, but one major thing she failed to do was acknowledge those in the audience who had helped work on the issue with her. It was a missed opportunity for her. It is important to look for those in the audience whom you can acknowledge, thank, or connect with. Mentioning someone's name and contribution is invaluable to gaining support for your initiatives while also building goodwill with the individual you recognize.

Before I speak, I always try to find connections to others in the audience. This often requires some preparatory research up front, but it pays dividends by enhancing the impact of the presentation and helping me gain support. The next time you need the help of these individuals, they will be likely to work extra hard for you. The rest of the audience will see you as a person who gives credit where credit is due.

Defining your audience and tailoring your message to their interests and needs may seem like a tall order, but it really sets you up for success when you translate your message into their language and their way of thinking.

A few years ago I was presenting to the senior management team at my company on handling the communication behind some environmental concerns. After what I thought was a good talk, I failed to get an approval in the room to move forward with my recommendations—instead they said they needed time to study them. Afterward, concerned, I asked a mentor who had been at the meeting what I could have done better.

"You threw everything but the kitchen sink at us," he replied frankly. "You could have gotten your message down to five key points instead of ten. There was so much technical information that you should have had one-on-ones with each of us ahead of time. This would have helped us understand the specifics, and at the meeting we might have been ready to approve your initiatives."

I learned two things from his comments. First, if you're communicating important technical information to a non-technical audience, presenting to a group straight out of the gate isn't the best choice. People have egos, and in a big group they will be reluctant to ask questions for fear of looking dumb. They'll act like they understand, even when they don't. The result? A disengaged audience.

Preparing beforehand with one-on-ones gives key individuals the opportunity to ask questions and engage in a two-way exchange in a nonthreatening setting. A big bonus is that this will give you the opportunity to ask directly for their support of your initiative.

After this speech and this feedback, I always give careful thought to preparing for presentations to any high-level audience. If a forthcoming meeting is on a technical topic, I make sure to avoid trying to deliver technical details to unprepped attendees. If the technical message is important, I make myself available to each and every key audience member in advance, so all of them come to the presentation already briefed and familiar with the specialized information. This takes work, but it is a good way to sell your idea and ensure support.

I also learned that, with this level of audience, less is not just more—less is best. I keep my content, however broad, to just three to five key points, the most critical items for that timetable and for that audience. If people want more information, they will ask questions. Communicating the essentials and taking care not to waste anybody's time is vital to standing out as a great communicator.

Finally, when I'm finished with a presentation, no matter how well I think the talk went, I find the organizers or someone whose opinion I trust, and ask: "Please give me feedback on one or two things I need to do to make this message more powerful." I listen, and I make sure to incorporate the good ideas in my next talk. This is especially helpful when you have to present the same topic to multiple constituencies.

Some of the best communicators develop a reliable gut instinct about their audience. They're good at feeling what's right, what their listeners want or need to hear. Even for these fortunately gifted speakers, however, there are times and situations when gut instinct is insufficient or simply fails entirely. By all means, listen to your gut and develop your instincts, but do not rely on them. Supplement the gut check by gathering the facts.

I've made the transition from frightened speaker to confident presenter because I was given this excellent advice to frame my thinking: public speaking is a learned skill, and anyone can learn it and become adept at it. It takes work—coaching, practice, knowing your material, and, most important, knowing your audience.

ASK QUESTIONS . . .

So far, we've been talking mostly about the "brand" messages you broadcast. But developing your personal brand is not all about one-way communication. It's highly interactive. Just as asking questions can help you engage an audience, it can also help you engage an individual. It's one of the best ways to show your smarts without being intimidating.

In our culture, beauty and intelligence are perceived as a rare combination, which can be intimidating to some people—especially men. You can turn this around to your advantage without having to play dumb. Never play dumb. The truth is that people—male or female—who make it their business to show off their expertise run the risk of being perceived as snobby, pedantic, or secretly insecure. Asking questions is much more effective than repeatedly trotting out your education for everyone to gawk at. Far from suggesting ignorance or stupidity, asking questions communicates your intellectual curiosity, which not only is the basis of high intelligence but also is generally perceived as such.

Never hesitate to ask questions in any business setting. It demonstrates to people that you have an interest in their work, and it builds your knowledge base, which will increase your value to your company. Incompetent, poorly educated, inadequately prepared, or just plain stupid people do not know enough to ask questions. I can tell you that, throughout my management career, one of the most important ways I evaluated top talent was by paying attention to who asked the best questions. The fact is that if *you* don't understand something, it is likely that you're not alone. So speak up, and ask your question.

Getting the answers will only make you more effective at your job. As a leader, you often depend on your employees to be the subject matter experts. If you can't ask incisive questions that cut to the heart of the matter, you'll find yourself at a major disadvantage.

Just as important as asking questions is never hesitating to ask for clarification when something said sticks in your craw or does not make complete sense to you. Accept nothing significant at face value, unless you fully understand the proposition. Knowledge really *is* power, and nowhere is knowledge more powerful than in business leadership. Women especially may be afraid to ask for clarification, fearing that colleagues will think they are uninformed or simply dense. Go ahead and ask for it with the same confidence with which you would ask any question. Never couch your query in an apology: "I'm sorry, but I just don't understand." Instead, put it positively: "I want to learn more about this." No one can fault you for that!

A big part of your brand should be *inquisitive, curious, questioning.* Asking questions not only brings clarity for yourself and others but also engages the people with whom you are communicating. It is a powerfully good thing to be identified as the woman who wants answers—who wants to learn—and who asks questions so that she can create and share solutions.

. . . AND TELL A STORY

Storytelling is another powerful means of engaging others. Too many managers communicate exclusively through orders, directions, and directives. These are important, but not especially interesting on what you might call a *human* level.

The Power of Parable

Storytelling is a powerful way for a leader to communicate in any number of situations. Use stories when . . .

- *Asking for money for a project.* Create a word picture of what the project will look like with the money, and then without. *Show* your audience the potential positive impact.
- *Giving feedback.* People don't generally like to hear their endeavors reduced to a list of abstract words or principles. Consider finding or creating an analogous story instead. Such a story will tend to make people less defensive than direct feedback.
- *Explaining a complex idea or process.* Vividly show how a given initiative drives value in the broader organization, and you will be more likely to win support. For example, I learned to focus on dollars, not bytes and bits, when telling an IT story outside of our department. Money is the universal language of business, and the more fluently you speak it, the more effectively you will move others to the actions you advocate.

Consider stepping up from giving mere instructions to sharing a really good tale.

If you were lucky enough to have a mother or father who told (or read aloud) bedtime stories, maybe you remember Aesop's fable "The North Wind and the Sun." It was one of my favorites. In the fable, the North Wind and the Sun compete to decide which of them is the stronger force. Looking down on a foot traveler, they agree to a test to see which of them can remove the man's cloak.

Naturally, it seemed obvious to the North Wind that he had the advantage in this contest. All he had to do was blow the garment from the man's shoulders. But the harder the North Wind blew, the more tightly the shivering traveler pulled his cloak about him against the cold. The North Wind having failed, the Sun's turn came. He took another approach altogether. Shining brightly, illuminating the traveler's way, he warmed the man so that, voluntarily, the traveler removed his cloak. Where the approach of cold, hard, brute-force coercion failed, the positive approach of gentle warmth and welcome light succeeded.

I first heard this fable decades ago, but the lesson has stayed with me all these years. The solution that gives rather than takes, that convinces instead of compels, usually works best— even though, quite often, this method requires out-of-the-box, counterintuitive thought and invention.

Telling stories helps you get your point across in a memorable way. It is important to put your concepts out there, but they are almost always most persuasive when wrapped in a story. It's hard to find a person who does *not* get absorbed in a really good story. We're naturally hungry for a compelling tale. So, wrap the abstract in the actual. Give examples. Relate anecdotes. Show the concept in action—where it happened and how it played out.

Stories are powerful vehicles of communication because, although they convey ideas, they are built on action, things, and feelings. They are human—as human as a smile. Much of our so-called "formal" education is conceptual in nature. Yes, concept and theory are undeniably important. Without conceptual and theoretical understanding, we would be doomed to operate pretty much exclusively by trial and error. Nevertheless, you, just like any business leader, must know how and when to step down from theory and get into the trenches of real-world experience. When you do, be sure that you know how to take your team with you. Get them into the action, the objects, and the emotions of business in the real world.

Dare to . . . Become Your Own Best Advocate

Chances are you are great at some of the skills discussed in this chapter and struggling with others. Review this checklist to identify the areas where you need to focus on self-improvement.

Do you . . .

✓ Get incredible results, both individually and through your team, and create opportunities to articulate those results to influencers in the organization?

✓ Extend your core integrity to life's small details, such as timeliness, courtesy, and a positive daily demeanor?

✓ Prioritize your mental and physical health, even when work and life are at their busiest?

✓ Negotiate your salary when starting a new job?

✓ Pursue raises when you know you deserve them, and at least annually?

✓ Find opportunities to speak publicly in front of large groups, inside and outside of your organization?

✓ Speak up and ask questions without worrying whether you "look stupid"?

✓ Communicate through storytelling rather than abstraction?

Once you've honestly evaluated yourself, pick the area that you think is most important to moving forward in your career, and make a commitment to making a "next step" to improve it—that might be reading a book, taking a class, scheduling a meeting, or signing yourself up for a speaking engagement. Whatever it is, make sure you follow through!

CHAPTER FOUR

DARE TO PROJECT A CONFIDENT ATTITUDE

Embrace the Behaviors and Mind-Sets of Powerful Leadership

Our doubts are traitors, and make us lose the ground we oft might win by trying to attempt.

WILLIAM SHAKESPEARE,
MEASURE FOR MEASURE, ACT I, SCENE 4

H aving self-confidence is the difference between feeling unstoppable and feeling scared out of your wits. What is more, your perception of yourself has a big impact on how others perceive you. The more self-confident you are, the more likely you will be to succeed.

I muddled through the early part of my career without much in the way of confidence, but I knew that if I wanted to go further, I'd need to change. In the early 1990s I faced my fears head-on when I was chosen to participate in the Program for Management Development at Harvard Business School. Business leaders from all over the world were invited to complete a "mini MBA" during a very intense four months on campus. This class had 120 global participants, sixteen of them women, the most that had ever attended in the program's thirty-plus years.

Although the caliber of my fellows was daunting, I had no problem participating vocally and without reserve in our small study group, in which I was the only woman. (They had distributed the women evenly throughout the groups.) Speaking before the full assembly was another story. During lectures, the men were very forceful in speaking up and ruthless in their challenges of each other. The women were completely intimidated. Actually, so were some of the men.

This became a subject of concern for the two female professors we had. When they called the women together to discuss it, we explained that we just weren't comfortable speaking up in a room filled with such aggressive, dominant male personalities. We didn't leave that discussion with any answers about how to overcome the problem.

Meanwhile, my study group decided to take on the issue. The others in my group became determined to get me to speak up in class, having seen that I was full of insight in our small group sessions. They were as concerned as our professors that women weren't speaking up. They sat next to me in class, pressuring me to raise my hand. They wouldn't quit.

Finally I relented. I was shaking in my seat, sure my voice would come out in a peep. But it didn't. It held strong and true as I articulated my point. When I was done, someone picked up my argument and added to it. I watched as my words changed the direction of the discussion, even the outcome of the case study we were developing. How liberating! I finally saw how much *power* my words could have—but only if I dared to raise my hand.

That realization changed me greatly. I became someone who was never again afraid to dare to share my thoughts or ask questions, even back at my company in which the cultural norm for both men and women at the time was to keep your mouth shut in public forums. The confidence I took home with me from Boston improved my career immeasurably.

The link between confidence and daring is easy to make: you're much more willing to take a leap from the solid foundation of a confident outlook than from the shifting sands of insecurity, in any stage of your life or career. Much of what you can achieve is determined by whether you believe you can achieve it. If you approach a challenge with the belief that it is impossible or that you're on the wrong path, you cannot focus on what you need to do to get the job done. If, however, you are confident that (or even just act as if) something is possible, you will tend to position yourself to attain the envisioned goal, even if you have to make multiple attempts.

Once you enter executive leadership, confidence only becomes more important. Although it may not be in the official job description, it's an absolute requirement. Executives typically have to make critical, wide-reaching decisions amid uncertainty, with less time for deliberation than they might have had earlier in their career. That requires a good dose of self-assurance. Once you make decisions, you need others to act on them. How others perceive you becomes much more important than it might have been in prior roles. Exude confidence, and people snap to attention.

Leadership is rarely endowed and often is something that must be taken. That said, working in an organization, you'll ultimately need someone to invite you into senior leadership. To get on the list, you'll need confidence to seize informal opportunities to take charge and put yourself forward as a change agent.

Allow me to fill you in on a secret: self-confidence is as much a learnable skill as it is a deep-seated character trait. That's good news, because all of the women featured in this book unanimously cited confidence as the quality most instrumental in their rise to the top.

There are three pillars underlying confidence: attitude, knowledge, and experience. We'll talk about how to maximize the latter two in the next chapters. Here we'll discuss mastering a confident *attitude,* exploring behaviors and mind-set shifts that will get you in the habit of acting and thinking from a place of power.

The Mentors Speak: On Building Confidence

When you are young, new business situations can be intimidating. If you expect to be accepted, however, you will walk into the room with a new level of comfort, a feeling that everyone will want to meet you, get to know you, and work with you. Then build your personal brand through hard work and delivering great results. Over time, when you meet new people, they'll say, "I've heard your name. It's great to finally meet you." Believe me, it happens. And it starts with expecting acceptance.

Joan Pertak, SVP and CIO, PepsiCo Americas Beverages and Quaker Foods and Snacks in North America

There is a tremendous amount of fear in the workplace, where people feel they aren't necessarily doing the right thing or saying the right thing to get ahead. In my experience people imagine there are more politics in the workforce than there actually are. I believe people need to turn their perspective around and recognize they have the capacity to control their own situation, or at least how they respond.

Rebecca Jacoby, CIO and SVP, IT and Cloud & Systems Management Technology Group, Cisco

Though I may feel "fear" in certain circumstances, I have learned to objectively deal with uncertainty and know that fear is most often an immediate emotional response to a lack of information or lack of control.

Karen Robinson Cope, SVP of sales and marketing, NanoLumens

Preparation builds confidence, whether you're an athlete who practices harder or an actor who rehearses longer. The same is true in business. If you are prepared, you are more likely to succeed, and success breeds self-confidence.

Kathleen Matthews, chief communications and public affairs officer, Marriott International

GET OVER YOUR NEED TO BE LIKED

Several times in my career I have been responsible for massive transformation efforts. These initiatives are always tough because they mean driving much-needed but often unwelcome change. People resist change and often aren't very happy with those who are "to blame" for it.

During one such effort, I was charged with reducing our corporate communications budget by 20 percent. I looked at what we could cut. In those pre-YouTube, pre-GoToMeeting days, we had our own internal TV network that executives could use to record and broadcast messages to everyone in the company. But no one liked the system, which forced people to drop what they were doing and leave their desks to go gather in a room to actually see these videos, sort of like a fire drill.

When I started looking at the TV network's budget, I found a $50,000 expenditure just to "encourage people to use it." Well, if we had to spend that much just to get people to use it, I didn't think we needed it at all. I advocated cutting the department entirely. We wouldn't fire anyone, but would move them to other departments. The twenty people who had been running this network were, needless to say, very, very unhappy with me, even when I explained we would find places for them elsewhere in the organization. As would happen many times in my career, they angrily questioned my judgment, arguing that I didn't know enough to be cutting their budget.

Their disapproval got to be so much that it was starting to affect my confidence in my actions. I called my father for some advice—and really just to vent. He gave me what turned out to be a great insight.

"Always remember that dogs don't chase parked cars."

Huh?

"You need to understand that if you are out front and driving change, you are going to have dogs chasing you," he explained. "Change makes people upset. You can't take it personally or let it distract you. Dogs don't chase parked cars."

In other words, if I knew I was doing the right thing, I should not be afraid, even if it meant a lot of barking at my back. As Margaret Thatcher once said, "If you just set out to be liked, you would be prepared to compromise on anything at any time, and you would accomplish nothing."[1]

For women especially, ignoring the barking can be challenging for a simple reason: generally speaking, we have been conditioned by our culture to want to be liked, so the state of each of our relationships is more prone to affect our self-esteem. Deborah Tannen's book *You Just Don't Understand: Women and Men in Conversation* explores patterns in men and women's communication styles.[2]

In it, Tannen lays out research supporting the idea that, whether by nature, nurture, or both, women predominantly live in a world of *connections*, whereas men live in a world of *status*. Women's identity and esteem are strongly connected to their relationships, and they seek out opportunities to enhance intimacy and connection. According to Tannen, women are comfortable taking orders rather than calling the shots when it serves to strengthen a relationship.

Obviously, these are generalizations, and people are rightfully wary of them because no one, woman or man, wants to be pigeonholed at work due to wrongheaded assumptions based on gender. That said, I've seen the concept at play and heard about it from enough female colleagues to believe it's worthwhile for every woman to examine herself and ask to what degree the need for approval and admiration is affecting her behavior in the workplace.

Here's how I've personally seen the need to be liked hurt women's careers. I have seen women back off too easily on any given issue because they don't want to make people angry or upset. I have seen women fail to speak up or present confidently to superiors due to extreme self-consciousness. I have watched women hesitate in firing someone because they dreaded facing the person's distress.

I have also seen men make all of these mistakes. But more often, it's the women.

There are obviously many positives for those of us who are more relationship oriented than status oriented, particularly in today's flattening, collaborative workplace. But we need to be aware of when our desire to be liked is keeping us from having the confidence and courage to take on challenging assignments, present our capabilities, deal with tough personnel issues, and push the envelope on our ideas.

Acting independently, whatever others think, could be even more difficult for the coming generation, as the young feminist blogger Jessica Valenti argues: "We're brought up to believe that our worth is tied to what others think of us. This is especially true for younger women today, whose every thought and action is made public on social media— literally waiting to be 'liked,' commented on, reblogged and affirmed by the world. Telling women to push all that aside—even if it is for long-term success and happiness—is no small thing."[3]

Hard as it may be, we've got to move past our fear of negative reactions if we want to be successful in promoting ourselves and our ideas. Genevieve Bos, the CEO of IdeaString, suggests building confidence by focusing on how your goals and ideas are serving the needs of others. "It's not just about you, it's about the contribution you make to others every day," she says. "Sometimes getting your mind off *you* and focusing on who you can be of service to with your unique gifts is a great way to build self-confidence."

HOW TO BE ASSERTIVE
WITHOUT BEING PUSHY

Losing your fear of being disliked doesn't mean pretending that "likeability" isn't important to workplace success. One of the great benefits of increasing your confidence is that it makes you more magnetic.

That said, "likeability" for women holds special challenges. Maybe you're familiar with Stanford professor Frank Flynn's famous "Heidi/Howard" experiment, conducted at Columbia University.[4] Flynn asked half of the students, male and female, to read a Harvard Business School case study of Silicon Valley investor Heidi Roizen. The other half read the identical case but were told that it was *Howard* Roizen. The students judged the male and female personae as equally capable, but those who had Heidi found her to be less likeable than the other half perceived Howard to be. Although only the gender was changed in Heidi's story, students' main complaint with her was that she seemed selfish.

Even today, women are more likely than men to be considered "pushy" by men *and* other women when displaying assertiveness or confidence. The surest route from *pushy* to *confident*, in terms of how you feel and how others perceive you, doesn't require you to soft-pedal or be overly solicitous. Instead, be as thorough and data driven as possible. Backing up your arguments with data protects you from personal attacks. If you can prove you're right, you'll win people's respect, even when it's grudging, and even when you're making bold demands. Further, people will be more receptive to your requests, proposals, and new ideas if you give them every reason to say yes. Do your research, articulate the wins clearly, and contextualize your argument according to their point of view.

I was never given advice on how to be direct and assertive without alienating people. I had to learn for myself, and what I came to realize was that there is a certain balance, a tough balance, you have to strike with people to get what you and your enterprise need from them. Sometimes you have to be creative and charm people with your smile and your graciousness while you firmly stand your ground. It's okay to be forceful, but never be unkind. It's hard for people to be ugly to someone who treats them with respect. Find ways to be both insistent *and* gracious.

Meanwhile, accelerate the process of building your confidence by actually *teaching* people how to treat you. Behave timidly, move hesitantly, and people will assume you lack confidence. Trust me, they will *not* respond by trying to bolster your confidence. Instead, they will treat you strictly according to your manifested lack of confidence. They *won't* listen to you. They *will* push you around. For these reasons, whether you feel confident or not, project confidence.

Avoid the reflexive use of "I'm sorry" as a conversation smoother, even if your intention is to communicate, "I'm sorry this happened to you." For example, when someone comes to retrieve her keys left behind on your desk, avoid saying, "*I'm so sorry*, here they are." Apologizing all the time telegraphs a lack of confidence, whatever its true meaning. I once received an e-mail response from a woman forty-eight hours after I'd sent an initial message to her. She spent the entire first paragraph apologizing for waiting so long to reply and explaining in great detail why the delay had happened. Meanwhile, it had seemed to me a reasonable response time in the first place. I was more troubled by the time I was wasting reading her long-winded apology!

DON'T BE *TOO* GRATEFUL

The language we use can influence people's perception of us— and perception is reality, especially when it comes to emotion and attitude.

In one of my previous roles, I was part of a corporate council that identified high-potential talent for a company in Atlanta. We reviewed background material on each candidate and then selected the most promising for interviews. At the time, I was the only female on the council, and I could not help but notice big differences in how male and female candidates introduced themselves. The guys walked in and said something to the effect of, "I got this interview because I'm good." The young women walked in and said something more like, "I'm so blessed to be here. I'm so grateful."

Blessed? Grateful? "You've gotten this far," I wanted to tell them, "because you're qualified and you're competent."

These women didn't seem capable of admitting as much. It would have been better for them to say, "Thank you for the opportunity to tell you more about myself."

Their comments—achievement equated with divine intervention or the kindness of strangers—came from a limited mind-set about what women believe they are permitted to have and do. It's a mind-set in desperate need of changing.

Driving this destructive mental orientation is a set of outmoded cultural traditions. Even among the most recent generation, there is a belief—inculcated in childhood—that certain behaviors are improper for a girl. Anything smacking of "aggression" is frowned on as too masculine. As females, we are more apt to have been taught to be passive rather than active.

Examine the language you use to talk about your achievements, and make sure it gives credit where credit is due—*to you.*

NEVER ACCEPT *NO* AT FACE VALUE

Sometimes we're afraid to ask for what we want because we're scared of getting shot down. Well, let's talk a minute about rejection. "No" does not always mean *no*. In other words, *no* need not end a negotiation. Often, that negative is tied to a particular time, set of circumstances, or understanding, which suggests its true meaning is closer to *maybe* than it is to *no*—and *maybe* can be very close indeed to *yes*.

So, don't be intimidated when someone tells you *no*, and certainly don't let a negative response undermine your confidence. Hearing *no* should simply challenge you to find another, more creative way to achieve the buy-in necessary to accomplish your goal.

A very talented employee on my team once exercised the initiative to tell me she wanted to move into a job that would give her experience outside of her current knowledge base. I liked the idea, but when I talked to the head of the department into which she wanted to rotate, he rejected the move out of hand. In his opinion, she was "too technical" to work in his area. Instead of walking away, I proposed to pay her salary while she worked in his area for six months, after which we would plan to take her back into our department. It was an offer he couldn't refuse, and *no* turned out to be *maybe*, which quickly slid over into *yes*.

Six months later, the department head was so impressed, he wanted to keep her. He not only was willing to pick up the cost of her salary but even included a slight increase. In business, no answer, including a negative answer, is final until you and the person you asked *both* agree it is.

MASTER THE 90 PERCENT RULE

To all of us—sometimes—the world seems out of control. The fact is, at any given time, much of the world *is* out of control, at least out of my control and yours. There's one thing, however, over which you always have power: your attitude. The more aware of your own attitude you become, the better you'll get at pushing it in a positive direction that creates confidence and supports daring.

Hala Moddelmog, the first woman to lead an international restaurant company as president of Church's Chicken, and who in 2010 became the president of Arby's, spoke to me about the importance of what she calls the 90 Percent Rule. "Life is 10 percent what happens to me and 90 percent how I react to it. Ninety percent of success is how you deal with the curveballs—those surprises and challenges that inevitably come our way," she says. "I believe it's important to maintain confidence and composure, and to stay calm when there is a problem. I try to understand the issue, put the facts on the table, pinpoint where the mistake happened, then brainstorm and work to fix the problem."

As the old saying goes, "Attitude determines altitude." A positive, open, *confident* attitude will boost you up any corporate ladder, whereas a negative, narrow, insecure attitude will just as surely drag you down and hold you there. At some point everyone encounters hard times, hurt feelings, heartache, and physical or emotional pain. The key is to remember it's not what happens to you that matters; it's how you respond.

To most of us, *attitude* means a state of mind. To an airplane pilot, however, the primary meaning of the word is the orientation of an aircraft's axes relative to the horizon. Consider your attitude from the pilot's perspective. Adopt a "good" attitude, and you will ascend. Fall prey to a "bad" attitude, and you will crash.

YOU'RE A FRAUD—AND SO IS EVERYONE ELSE

Our minds are powerful tools. Our thoughts and emotions guide our behavior, and neurologists have demonstrated that we process thoughts many times faster than we can speak them. Research suggests we can speak at about 150 to 200 words per minute while simultaneously thinking to ourselves at the rate of some 1,300 words per minute.[5] Without even being consciously aware of it, we continually convince ourselves that we can or cannot do something. These thoughts shape the attitudes that translate into action or inaction. It's incredibly important, therefore, that you're "feeding" yourself the right thoughts! That means identifying the attitudes that are most crippling to confidence, recognizing them for what they are—*thoughts*, not reality—and then replacing them with more positive messages.

So, what are the most common offenders when it comes to destructive thinking? Where to begin! Millions of years of evolution have programmed humans for a level of caution that was once critical to survival. Our instinct, as both men and women, is to protect ourselves from possible harm, and the conversations we silently hold with ourselves consist for the most part of one warning after another.

As humans, we are programmed to remember harmful events. Our brains are like Velcro for negative experiences and Teflon for positive ones—even though most of our experiences are probably neutral or positive.[6] Negative events generally have more impact than positive ones. For example, it's easy to acquire feelings of learned helplessness from a few failures, but hard to undo these feelings, even with many successes.[7] In relationships, it typically takes about five positive interactions to overcome the effects of a single negative one.[8]

Good things are happening all around us, but much of the time we don't notice them. You must make the conscious choice to acknowledge the positive things around you. By doing so, you can change your outlook and attitude, making yourself more open to new opportunities.

Failure to dare certainly isn't limited to women, but we seem to have a special propensity for it. I have watched so many women, including myself, wrestle with what psychologists describe as *imposter syndrome*. Many of today's most powerful women—Tina Fey, Maya Angelou, and even Sheryl

Sandberg—admit to having suffered from some version of the condition. It was first described by Pauline Rose Clance and Suzanne Imes in 1978 as an "internal experience" among many women, who, despite "outstanding academic and professional accomplishments," believe "that they are really not bright and have fooled anyone who thinks otherwise."[9]

Imposter syndrome is not a mental illness. In fact, it may be deemed a "normal" condition, considering that 70 percent of individuals are estimated to have experienced it at some point during their lives. But it seems to affect more women than men, and psychologists have found this syndrome to be especially prevalent among women who have chosen to pursue traditionally male professions—or at least those professions perceived to be best suited to men. Women in science, technology, engineering, and mathematics (STEM) careers, for example, are particularly vulnerable to feeling unworthy, especially because they often see themselves as pioneers who have taken on the heavy burden of representing their gender in a male-dominated field.

The feelings associated with the syndrome are real, and they can be painful. But to get past it, the goal doesn't have to be conquering the feeling that you're a fraud, although that certainly will help. The better solution might in fact lie in embracing those feelings while creating a system that allows you *to act anyway.*

"Fake it till you make it" may not be poetry worthy of Shakespeare, but it's a pretty sturdy formula for career progress. If you are going to wait until you feel ready to act with confidence, you are in for a very long wait—longer than you or your career can afford. You don't really have to be perfect or perfectly self-assured before you set out to build your success. But you do have to roll up your sleeves and dig into the job of creating both the opportunity and ability to dare.

Genevieve Bos, a successful serial entrepreneur who currently is the CEO of IdeaString, an online collaboration and ideation platform, also experienced imposter syndrome early in her career. "For years, I was afraid to show that I did not know a thing," she told me. "I was afraid that if I asked too many questions, people I worked with would think I was a fraud. I spent so many years hiding in plain sight. It's the feeling that you are not good enough, smart enough, capable enough to achieve higher levels."

Genevieve has moved past those anxieties. Her attitude changed after she joined the peer coaching group Entrepreneurs Organization, and found herself surrounded by hundreds of hugely successful entrepreneurs, mostly men, who talked openly about their vulnerabilities. "I finally realized that acknowledging what you are great at and not so great at is a huge strength, and in fact is the basis for empowering yourself and others to achieve," she says. "All the incredible wasted stress and worrying was time I could have been focusing on what was most important."

Another remedy may lie in shifting from a "fixed" mind-set to a "growth" mind-set. Stanford University psychologist Carol Dweck describes this paradigm in her book *Mindset: The New Psychology of Success.* Dweck looks at the historical debate among scientists and philosophers over whether a person's intellectual makeup and character are defined by nature or nurture, and concludes, along with Alfred Binet, the inventor of the IQ test, that "it's not always the people who start out the smartest who end up the smartest."[10]

Many people don't approach their careers with that mind-set; rather, they have a *fixed mind-set,* according to Dweck: "Believing that your qualities are carved in stone . . . creates an urgency to prove yourself over and over. If you have only a certain amount of intelligence, a certain personality, and a certain moral character—well, then you'd better prove that you have a healthy dose of them. It simply wouldn't do to look or feel deficient in these most basic characteristics."[11]

One can see fairly easily how the fixed mind-set could make it difficult for you to dare with confidence. What could be more paralyzing to the fixed mind-set, for example, than taking on a stretch role in which you know you'll need to learn in the moment; on the job; in the plain gaze of all the people reporting to you, and no doubt your bosses, too?

If you can cultivate a *growth mind-set,* you'll no longer see every challenge as a harrowing proof point of your potential (or, in your clumsier moments, lack thereof). Rather, these are welcome opportunities to show that you're constantly growing and learning.

FORGE A MIDDLE PATH

Another limiting mind-set I've seen often in the women I work with is zero-sum thinking, particularly when it comes to the elusive question of how to "balance" work and family life. Many think that motherhood is irrevocably incompatible with the demands of corporate leadership. Without a doubt, this is something that highly successful women, and increasingly men alike, struggle with. I'm not going to tell you it's easy.

Beverly Daniel Tatum, whom you met in Chapter One, initially felt like she might have to stand down from the selection process for Spelman College's presidency because it would mean moving her husband and son at a potentially deleterious moment for both of them. Once she decided it was what she really wanted, however, not only did her husband and son support her but also they came up with a plan that worked for all of them. It required sacrifice, but one they felt was worth it so that Beverly could make an impact at the very top of her field.

Robin Bienfait was the CIO of Research In Motion and had responsibility for overseeing the enterprise business unit, BlackBerry operations, and corporate IT until her retirement in 2013. Earlier in her career, Robin was offered a position she had always wanted that would finally allow her to make the jump from middle to senior management. "All weekend long, I wrestled with the decision," she says. "My husband and I had a tough time deciding if we should move the family across the country so I could accept the promotion. In the end, we decided it was both too much work to move and not the right fit." When Monday came, she declined the offer. Not two hours later, Robin got a call from the hiring team offering her the very same job—and in her hometown.

Robin was lucky to work for a company that knew her value and was willing to compromise to count her among its leadership. Clearly, the leverage of excellence helps here. But too many women back down from pursuing senior management because they think they'll be forced to choose, *my career* or *my family*. Who knows what opportunities may prove available when we demand them. Says Robin, "Sometimes you need to know when to walk away from something, and to be certain that the career moves you make are truly good for you *and* your family. . . . Don't sacrifice your happiness. Nothing is worth that." The importance of holding out for the right fit and making your needs known can never be overstated.

THE NETWORK EFFECT

Once you start to understand the mind-sets that are influencing your behavior, it immediately becomes much easier to manage them. Studies conducted by Dweck and others have actually shown this to be the case. But for mind-sets and biases you just can't seem to move confidently past, rely on others to help you. Find people you trust who exemplify success and smart decision making. When your inner voice is screaming, "It's too hard," "Why risk it?" or "Say no," reach out for the opinion of these trusted individuals.

In general, the people with whom you interact will have an incredible effect on your attitude and outlook. For example, social contagion theorists Nicholas Christakis and James Fowler have posited based on their studies that each happy friend you add to your circle increases your own probability of being happy by about 9 percent.[12] It is in your best interest—and in the best interest of your team—to associate with individuals who possess positive, confident attitudes, and to be on guard against people whose toxic attitudes can drain *your* energy as well as theirs.

Associate with a crowd that is habitually negative and unsure, and the next thing you know, you'll be one of them, your attitude transformed from ascending to spiraling downward, your vision hemmed in by the ever-approaching horizon. One of the best things you can do if you want to be a good tennis player is to play with someone better than you. Attitudes are the same. If you want to become more positive, more confident, more hopeful, hang out with others who embody those attitudes.

Likewise, remember that your attitude makes an impact on those around you. People gravitate to positive, confident people. This includes subordinates, whose work is necessary to your success, and supervisors, who can advise and support you. Your ability to attract the best talent to help you with your assigned project or your long-term goals is directly tied to your attitude.

Try This Experiment!

Find someone with a sour expression. Flash him or her a smile and a "Hey, how're you doing?"

Observe.

Almost always, you'll see the other person's expression soften and then broaden into a return smile. This is "emotional contagion." (It won't happen 100 percent of the time. A few people seem to be immune. Nevertheless, in more than thirty-three years in management, I've only encountered a handful of people who just would not—or could not—smile back.)

AWAKEN THE VOICE
OF AMBITION

Leadership is taken, not given. This is true for men, and even more urgently true for women. Finding the confidence to rise up and move ahead is hard, but no one said that *taking* leadership would be easy. If your thoughts can drive you to achieve the amazing, they can also turn you into your own worst enemy. Self-doubt and negative thoughts can muzzle the ambitious voice inside you and easily deter you from pursuing your own success.

To overcome self-doubt, first acknowledge your fears and your negative mind-sets. Don't try to pretend they don't exist; however, having admitted them, refuse to live in obedience to them. Refer back often to the vision and values you've outlined and let them be your guide. When doubt says, "I can't," reply, "I can." Repeat as necessary to build a belief that you can be successful; then put this belief at your very core.

As you reshape your attitude and step into behavior that takes you out of your comfort zone, you will probably feel at first like you're wearing new shoes that pinch at every step. My advice is simple: *keep on walking until you break them in.* Being the "first" woman in your company to crack the executive suite, or even just one of few, requires courage, constant growth, and comfort with risk. While you mature as a leader, you'll need to put on one new, pinching pair of shoes after another.

As you become comfortable with each new pair, your confidence will grow commensurately. The need for constant mental gymnastics of positive self-talk and affirmations will fade away, replaced by a voice inside telling you that you possess the tools and the skills to handle any challenge. A confident attitude and the language and actions that telegraph it to others will flow naturally. The concept of change, so uncomfortable at first, will become a habit. You'll accept fear as something that comes with a career, and rise above it.

Dare to . . . Own Your Attitude

Here is some practical advice for getting and keeping a more positive, productive, confident attitude:

Practice Saying Yes

Say yes to new challenges, even when your internal voice tells you to say no. Eventually you will find that you are actually thinking *yes* instead of your habitual thoughts of *no*. Reject the attitude that assumes a task is impossible until proven otherwise. Instead, adopt the mental and emotional position that assumes possibility until definitively proven impossibility.

Cultivate Positivity

- *Start each day with an activity you enjoy.* It is easier to maintain a positive attitude if you start the day off in a positive way.
- *Practice gratitude.* Remember what you have to be grateful for. Too many times we make comparisons to other people who have more than we do. If you focus instead on those less fortunate, chances are your attitude will be more positive.
- *Take breaks to smile and laugh.* Even forced laughter has been shown in several studies to have a short-term impact on mood.
- *Do something nice for someone.* It will make *you* feel better.
- *Eat a healthy diet and exercise.* Exercise releases neurotransmitters in the brain that decrease stress and enhances our mood.
- *Clean out and organize your work space.* Poor lighting and confusing clutter can really affect your attitude.
- *Hang out with positive people.* Invest your time in positive group activities.
- *Make a list of positive things that have happened to you.* Include goals you have achieved, compliments from others, things you have enjoyed, and past successes. Review the list often.

Monitor Your Self-Talk

Once you have identified negative internal messages, make a note when one crosses your mind. Substitute it with something positive: "Yes, I can."

Keep a journal with one sentence each day that describes your attitude. Review the journal frequently. Reading what you've written can give you a totally different perspective—especially if some time has passed.

Don't Rely on Negative Energy to Motivate You

We sometimes go out of our way to create deadlines, crises, and problems to fill up our day. Shift your motivation from avoiding pain to seeking pleasure. Instead of focusing on a deadline, think about the pleasure of accomplishing a task and what you may learn in the process.

Keep your vision statement and core values close at hand, referring to them when your energy is flagging.

Project a Confident Attitude

One of the most important things you can do to project confidence is to take action. The more you do something, the more comfortable it gets. Once people start noticing your new confidence, their response will reinforce and reward your hard work.

The following list of actions will get you started:

- *Do your homework.* Have the facts of a situation before entering into an important meeting or conversation. Seek input from others up front. Nothing will help you feel more confident than knowing that you have thoroughly researched an issue. A command of objective facts will take a lot of subjective emotion out of any issue, thereby making difficult decisions easier.

- *Create a professional image.* Dress your best, practice good posture, make eye contact, lead with a handshake, offer your name first, and smile. Looking professional affects the way you carry yourself and the way you interact with others.

- *Breathe deep.* Taking deep breaths increases oxygen saturation in your blood to feed the brain, allowing you to relax, feel confident, and focus. Although just 2 percent of your body weight, your brain uses roughly 20 percent of your oxygen. By taking several deep breaths, you increase oxygen saturation in your blood, and this revs up your brain.[13] Breathing exercises are easy to learn, and you can do them anywhere.

- *Sit in the front row in meetings.* This will make you more visible to the important people speaking—and it will keep you more alert.

- *Ask engaging questions and speak up in meetings.* Even people who ask great questions are often reluctant to speak up because they fear being judged by others. In reality, people interested enough in a topic to attend a meeting or conference are far more accepting of input from others than you might imagine. They actually tend to admire those who speak up, and they are often grateful for the perspective that engaging questions provide. By cultivating the habit of speaking up, you build public speaking skills and become increasingly confident about your own ideas. You also build recognition as a leader among your peers.

- *Seek out positive role models.* Hang around the right people. Choose those who share your goals and who have demonstrated success in attaining them—even more success than you enjoy. Do your best to identify and eliminate relationships that are downright toxic.

- *Compliment other people.* Doing so is a confidence builder for *you* even as it makes other people feel good about themselves and about you. Looking for the best in others brings out the best in us.

- *Focus on your contribution.* Looking beyond ourselves to how what we do benefits others builds self-confidence and defeats feelings of isolation.

- *Create a personal advertisement.* This is a statement that takes no more than a half-minute or minute to say (150 to 200 words), and that distills your accomplishments, strengths, and goals. Prepare it, then always be ready to deliver it. It's your personal, portable elevator pitch.

- *Write down your goals.* Set specific targets for yourself, such as becoming the CEO or CIO. Visualize these goals' becoming reality, then take the steps to make them happen.

- *Build a strong network of peers you can count on.* Build it within your organization, your industry, and your community.

- *Practice.* When you will be presenting to a group of any size, do a trial run beforehand and practice, practice, practice so you speak with confidence and fewer awkward pauses.

CHAPTER FIVE

DARE TO LEARN AT EVERY AGE

Become a Knowledge Seeker to Maintain Your Competitive Edge

Leadership and learning are indispensable to each other.
JOHN F. KENNEDY

"The best way to build self-confidence is to build knowledge," says Adriana Karaboutis, global chief information officer at Dell. "Learn, learn, learn. . . . Know your subject matter and be able to talk about it."

Knowledge is the second pillar of confidence, after attitude. It means knowing what you don't know as well as what you do, and it is critical to every leader. So many of the women I interviewed cited cultivating knowledge as foundational to their confidence. The deeper our knowledge, the more we feel we have the right to call the shots, even when others dispute our choices. The more we know, the more unknown variables we can handle confidently—and the more we feel our steps into the unknown are calculated risks, not reckless gambles.

The trouble is, keeping on the cutting edge of knowledge has never been more difficult. The pace of change is accelerating in every aspect of life, and nowhere faster than in business. Just look at my field, information technology. In

1978, at the start of my career, the Internet existed, but it was still against the law to use it for commerce, a fact that didn't officially change until 1995, which seems unimaginable now. Mobile technology and social media have similarly transformed the ways that companies interact with their customers, competitors, and vendors.

Knowledge is more dynamic than ever before, and much of what you need to know as a senior leader you won't find in a textbook or employee manual. In these days of relentless change, all true business leaders must be consummate students to stimulate and sustain both personal growth and growth in their organization.

Leaders today must train themselves to learn every day and evolve as the world around them changes and invites further change—change they must lead. As a leader, you have to be prepared to pivot, to try something entirely new, even though it means jumping back into a steep learning curve. It's up to you to use every available tool to find and process the information you need to keep yourself not just current, but always looking forward. Doing so also arms you with the confidence you need to stand up, speak persuasively, and get heard.

I'm also going to let you in on the secret to developing the kind of smarts you need to be an executive leader: you have to understand the mantra of the socially networked age, *nobody is as smart as everybody*. Every colleague and every employee is your teacher. For this reason, how you manage your relationships is more important than it has ever been before—a single employee or customer may be your best or even your only source for receiving a particular kind of information, so it's up to you to keep the conduit open.

If you truly want to stay at the edge of knowledge in your business and your organization—which you must, to keep your career and your team hurtling forward—you need a knowledge network, optimized to deliver the information you require, when you need it.

The Mentors Speak: On Learning

Pursue diversity aggressively. Take international opportunities; take roles outside of the traditional career path, even in totally different industries. Success in the future will be gained by people who are flexible, are curious, and have multiple experiences. The world of business is changing so rapidly that the skill of adapting and learning quickly, and, most important, *enjoying* that experience, will become premium in the new economy.

Penny McIntyre, former president,
Consumer Group, Newell Rubbermaid

Embracing change is a phrase we often hear, but actually doing it is critical. After spending fifteen years in IT, I came back to the States from a European assignment and moved—cross-functionally—into a business role, running production control at Ford Motor Company. It was a huge challenge, but also the best IT experience I ever had. Being an IT customer for six years better prepared me to become a stronger IT professional. Until you've walked in the customer's shoes, you don't fully appreciate the value of great systems and strong customer focus.

Adriana Karaboutis, VP and global CIO, Dell

Wake up, put your shoes on, and go out into the world and try stuff. If you don't know what to try, just go where people are, talk to them, listen, and be curious about what they do, and why they do what they do. You'll find something that interests you and that ignites a spark.

Kat Cole, president, Cinnabon

WHAT GOT YOU THERE WON'T GET YOU HERE

One of the most career-advancing moves I ever made was accepting a demotion—and not even one step down the ladder but two.

At the time, I had been working for twelve years in the finance area of my company and was on the high-potential leadership track in my department. Meanwhile, my instinct told me that finance wasn't the right place for me in the long term. I started looking for jobs in other departments, but each time, I was turned down. Although I was perceived as technically very competent, I was told that there were questions about my ability to work in roles that required interpersonal skills.

That's not feedback that anyone wants to hear, but I forced myself to listen. Even though I suspected "interpersonal skills" really meant "manly skills," I also hadn't had a role that really allowed me to demonstrate such skills. But I personally believed that these were the best skills I had, and so I knew that I needed an opportunity to prove I was capable.

I had long been fascinated by the work in our business development department, so I decided to meet directly with its leader. He told me I would most likely need to take a demotion if I wanted to enter his department, because I lacked any background in business development.

At the time, my company didn't have a development program in which employees could rotate into different areas and receive new experience. Moreover, the company had never put a woman in business development. Some of my peers even insisted that a woman couldn't do that type of work, because it would require her to wine and dine a bunch of men. If that sounds crazy, you have to realize that a decade earlier, the only roles for women in this company were as secretaries and as home economists, the women who went to people's homes to teach them how to use electric appliances. Company policy required these women to quit when they married. A lot had changed already.

Obstacles or no, when a position I thought appropriate opened up in the department, I threw my name in the hat and was offered the job. As the department head had warned me, it was two levels down from the role I previously held.

The prospect of breaking away from my established role in finance was really, really scary. I would be leaving the comfort and security of the fast track in the finance department and moving, at a lower level, into the more volatile world of business development. Instead of being a technical expert, I would be a novice. But then again, that was exactly the point—to learn something completely different. So what that I was twelve years into a finance career? If I wanted to be recognized for my interpersonal skills, I needed to be in a position where I could demonstrate them.

I did a lot of homework and asked many people for input. I was fortunate to have one of the senior leaders for a mentor, and he assured me this was a vital move if I were going to go further in my career. There weren't a lot of people in our company who had traveled outside of their functional silo to get a broader view. Getting that broad view from a totally new perspective would build my knowledge base and make me a more effective leader. He also reminded me that we're always more productive when we're doing something in which we believe we can grow, learn, and feel passion for the work.

So I did it. Many of my peers were shocked, and said as much. The first couple of months after the move were rough. First of all, business development folks used totally different language. Instead of talking about things like "return on equity," they were throwing around terms like "square footage" and "infrastructure." Second, I had to develop new networks, in my new division and, for the first time, outside of the company. I had so much to learn. At times, I thought I had made a terrible mistake. But then, after those initial months, I began to feel more comfortable in and more excited about the new role. I became increasingly confident in my ability to make a difference and be successful, to a degree I had never felt in finance.

Ultimately, the move got me noticed by our CEO, and proved to be one of the most pivotal decisions of my career. Several years later I was sent back to run the very division I was initially discouraged from joining.

Today, being prepared to pivot—five, ten, even twenty-five years into your career—is more important than ever to your long-term career trajectory. Business changes rapidly, so you have to dedicate yourself to staying sharp, adapting to new norms, and being competitive. The danger is falling into the mind-set that you've done everything that can be done. The world changes around you every second. Stand still, and you will be left behind. Many of today's hottest jobs did not exist ten years ago.

You may find it useful to start thinking of yourself as a product. Are you the latest thing—up to date and then some? Or are you getting a bit shopworn? How do you stack up against competing products? I used to require all my employees to choose a skill or subject area to develop and report back to me regularly. So many of them balked, saying they didn't have time. I told them exactly what I'm now telling you: continuing your learning throughout your career is something you can't afford *not* to do. Make it a priority.

Repeatedly design, redesign, and remanufacture yourself. Know your product. This begins with assessing what knowledge you have now and what knowledge you need, and then deciding how to apply both in your job.

Although I can't overemphasize the power of pivoting, I also want to stress that deep knowledge of your industry and function can also be key in preparing you for success at higher levels, where, as Southern Company's former executive VP of engineering and construction services, Penny Manuel says, "senior management expectations are both broad and deep." She was told early on by a mentor to "make sure she got her major" to develop deep expertise in one area. In her case, that meant spending ten years as a power plant engineer before moving to middle-management positions in several divisions. The first ten years were spent amassing deep subject area knowledge, and the second ten gave her insight into the broader workings of the corporation, "management intuition," and relationships across the company. She considers both decades to have been essential in laying the foundation for her first executive experience.

One of the most clear-cut ways to redesign "Product You" is through formal education. Advanced training and coursework can easily double or triple your income, and companies are investing heavily in executive education to stay competitive. It can also reengage you when you feel like your career is stagnating or stale. After having worked for twenty-five years as an anchor and reporter for ABC News TV in Washington DC, Kathleen Matthews started to feel as though she was phoning it in. "The work I had loved was no longer the challenge or the thrill that had kept me motivated and excited. I loved the storytelling, interviewing people, investigating tough, topical issues, but the stories were repeating themselves."

Not sure what to do or how to repurpose her skills, Kathleen applied for the Institute of Politics fellowship at Harvard's Kennedy School of Government and convinced ABC to give her a six-month sabbatical to take classes and teach a seminar about the changing media landscape. "What I learned at Harvard was that my skills were infinitely portable. Framing a news story had taught me about framing a business or political strategy. Understanding headlines had taught me how to envision goals and outcomes in a compelling way," she says.

The experience opened her eyes for the first time to the idea of a job outside of journalism. Soon enough, seemingly out of the blue, Marriot International came knocking, asking her to head up its Global Communications and Public Affairs department. She had never worked in business, never worked in marketing, never managed a staff. That said, the benefits were obvious—"international travel and a chance to stretch my skills and be reborn in a second career." Still fresh with the sense of possibility, competence, and renewed passion she felt while on sabbatical, Kathleen dared.

WHERE KNOWLEDGE MEETS CONFIDENCE

Jeanette Horan, who has served as IBM's CIO since 2011, told me a great story about how arming herself with knowledge made it possible for her to accomplish the most challenging feat of her career: having the confidence to convince IBM's entire senior executive team in 2006 that the Architecture and Standards division needed an entirely different approach if it wanted to keep up with the company's changing business strategy.

"There was a strong belief that we could make incremental progress, building on our legacy environment," says Jeanette. Over the course of nine months, she put together a thoroughly researched, fact-based business case that added up to the need for sweeping change. "Gathering the facts was very important in making the senior executives understand that staying on the prior course was not going to deliver the business result we needed. Once we had made that case, I knew I had an audience willing to listen." She won them over, and then spent three years leading the implementation of her recommendations across the organization—an even more difficult feat.

It's much easier to be bold and to resist backing down when you know the facts are on your side thanks to a thorough inquiry. Being "thorough" may require getting away from your desk and taking a look at the challenge you're troubleshooting from the perspective of a different industry or constituency. After thirty years as a civil servant in the Indian government, Loveleen Kacker knew she had a lot to learn to prepare for a new job in the social enterprise sector. But it wasn't just knowledge about the inner workings of her new organization that was needed. "I spent time visiting less privileged areas, and volunteering to get firsthand knowledge about the lives of the people I served," she says. She wanted to make sure she understood the social challenges she'd be working to overcome. She also thought she should look beyond the nonprofit space for potential solutions, and enrolled in two courses on corporate social responsibility. Finally, she met with the corporate social responsibility heads of several different companies.

"Only when I was sure I had learned all that I could did I start making changes in our office, setting performance targets and so on. When discussions were held concerning our pro-grams, I was on top of the situation, and I had the confidence to present a cogent and informed rationale for whatever I pro-posed," says Loveleen, who today is the CEO of the Tech Mahindra Foundation, the corporate social responsibility effort

---

Leading with a Knowledge Gap

As a leader, you'll frequently find yourself in charge of projects for which you have a substantial knowledge gap. Anesa Chaibi, presi-dent and CEO of HD Supply Facilities Maintenance, once had to lead a technical team of electrical engineers twenty to thirty years her senior to develop, design, and produce a new product to serve the power generation industry. "I did not feel very confident that I understood the technical elements that were critical to the success of the position, product, and company," she says. Nevertheless, the team developed a quality product and delivered it to market in only nine months, "a very aggressive cycle time for a highly engineered product and a significant accomplishment." Anesa offers these tips for leading when you have a knowledge gap:

- Immerse yourself in learning the technical aspects to build competence, understanding, and confidence to lead the team.
- Stand your ground when being tested or challenged by mem-bers of the team to establish credibility and authority as the leader.
- Never let your frustration show, and constantly remind yourself that failure is not an option.

of a multinational IT outsourcing company. She is the highest-placed female in the company. Says Loveleen, "No matter what area you work in, learn about it, experience it, and endeavor to improve your skills. Learn, and you will never lack confidence."

CULTIVATE NETWORK INTELLIGENCE

If you're a woman who excels at any of those stereotypically "female" skill sets that emphasize relationships and collaboration over status games, you may actually have a significant leg up on your male peers when it comes to knowledge development at the executive level.

As a senior leader, your responsibility becomes so broad that no matter how intelligent you are or how much you prepare, you can't possibly know everything. Add to that the speed of change in today's high-tech, global business environment, and the wisdom for decision making is no longer just about what's inside your head. It starts to be about what knowledge you can *inspire others to share with you.*

John Hagel is the founder, with John Seely Brown and Lang Davison, of the Deloitte Innovation Center for the Edge, a research group that lists helping executives to "learn faster" and "act boldly" among its goals. As such, they're experts on organizational learning in the age of technology. In describing the unique challenge of keeping ourselves at the edge of knowledge today, Hagel has said that the "old way" companies handled knowledge was to develop it, hoard it, and then tap its value by turning it into products and services. Now that the world is changing so rapidly, the value of that proprietary knowledge depreciates just as fast, so we need to be smarter, faster. "As a result of this new set of circumstances we now need to ask," says Hagel, "How do I participate in a broader, more diverse range of flows of knowledge so that I can refresh my knowledge stocks at an increasing rate?"[1]

Hagel's question is complex, but at least part of the answer lies in two increasingly important skills. First, executives—and really, all knowledge workers—need to be able to develop networks that readily provide quality information and expertise, even as missions and conditions change on a dime. And second, they need to create the kinds of relationships that encourage people in those networks to share freely and comfortably.

What kind of network will provide the best information? Cast a wide net. One of the ways we tend to limit the ideas and experience we can draw on is by interacting with the same small group of people all the time. The more diverse you can make your network, especially those to whom you typically go for career advice and information, the better. Think of diversity broadly—beyond age, gender, and social background, to industry and function. If you're like most people, you tend to gravitate toward people who dress, act, and think a lot like you do. There's nothing truly sinister about that. First of all, it can take effort to cultivate relationships outside of your company or immediate friend circle, so it's easy to get in a rut. It's also just instinct. "Prejudice is simply part of being human," wrote Keith Ferrazzi. "Thousands of years ago, rapid-fire assessments of 'friend or foe?' probably saved our ancestors' lives."[2] But the cave days are over. If you're only interacting with people who are immediately within your comfort zone, you're limiting the diversity of information that comes your way and missing an important opportunity for growth. Work on it.

And speaking of your comfort zone, make sure you're constantly seeking out relationships with people who challenge you. Tena Clark, who started her own company, DMI Music and Media Solutions, after a successful producing career, had a great answer when I asked for her best advice on making the leap from middle to senior management: "Don't play with someone at your level if you want to get better. If you surround yourself with mediocre people, you will be mediocre," she said. "The minute you think you know it all, you can put a sign saying *closed* on your door. You're done. You must keep learning and keep seeking advice—good, bad, and ugly. Surround yourself with lots of mentors." (For more on finding mentors, see Chapter Seven.)

IT'S NOT WHOM YOU KNOW, IT'S WHO TRUSTS YOU

Once you've created a diverse network, the next challenge is to become practiced in drawing information out of that network—whether it's your team, your group of contacts on LinkedIn, or your extended family. William Taylor, the cofounder of *Fast Company*, likes to ask the question, "What's your architecture of participation?" In other words, how are you opportunistically and systematically encouraging the people you work with to share?

It's critical to get feedback from everyone to formulate the best decisions. I made a point of stopping by each of my employees' offices face-to-face to ask, "What could I do better to make it easier for you to do your job? What do we need to change?" At one point I started hearing from a number of people, "We need more focus on leadership development." So I pulled together a small budget for a program. We didn't spend much but had tremendous success. As a result, people in our department started getting promoted, and we got a reputation as being one of the best areas of the company to work—which meant we attracted people of a higher caliber. And it all started because I asked questions and I listened to the answers. Open yourself up to the knowledge of the people who work for you—they often know more than you do about an issue at hand.

Sharing information quickly and openly positions your team for success. As an officer in my company, I made it a habit to leave my scheduling calendar open for everyone to see. I wanted my team to know where I was and what I was doing. In return, I wanted them to share with me what they were doing.

By making my appointments public knowledge, I ensured that my team saw when a senior-level meeting was approaching. Armed with this information, they always scrambled to get me the necessary information beforehand. For my part, I took notes at those meetings and shared them with the group. I felt prepared, and they were informed.

Many other executives were aghast at this level of transparency, but I trusted my team because I knew that the benefits outweighed the risks. Openly sharing that information led to better outcomes. Further, giving my team this level of access set a tone that made them comfortable to speak their mind about serious issues—I knew they weren't afraid to tell me something I didn't yet know, or to disagree with me. Knowledge was constantly flowing in my direction.

Trust is vitally important to learning. Being systematic about pulling information from your team, from other divisions, and from your broader network is important, but trust is the softer, more subtle side of effectively teasing knowledge from others.

Jeannette Horan, the IBM CIO, hinted at the trust factor in telling me how she succeeds when she assumes a new role that takes her beyond her expertise. "Whether you are building on your academic credentials or branching out into a new field, it is always important to listen," she says. "You don't have to know everything when you come into a new role, but it is important to quickly learn whom you can trust." Being able to evaluate who on your team can be trusted to provide information that's relevant and accurate is a key leadership skill. There aren't really any shortcuts in good executive decision making, but simply knowing whom to trust might come close.

You've also got to cultivate others' trust in you. I once had a boss who was brilliant, truly one of the most intelligent people I've ever worked with. The problem was that he walked around thinking everyone else was stupid. I once saw him shout a woman out of his office with a stream of expletives because she had said something he perceived as dumb. Do you think I ever *once* had the urge to risk adding a nuance, an additional fact, or, heaven forbid, a countervailing point to anything he proposed? Not even a little bit.

"But I'd never do that!" you might be thinking. Okay. Now imagine a boss who is respectful, but who has a leadership style that suggests that *she's* the one with the expertise. That's very easy to do as a boss. It's our job, after all, and why we're paid so handsomely. In addition, as women, depending on our industry, there may have been times when we had to jump hurdles to be taken seriously, and that has its effect. But watch out, because even *that* boss will quickly shut down her direct reports, and quite possibly her peers; it doesn't take yelling and cursing. If we want our employees to feel their point of view is important, and to take the time and initiative to explore, develop, and report back on their new ideas, we have to consciously send the message that we don't know everything, and that we welcome their input. In fact, why not make it explicit? In meetings and one-on-ones, just go ahead and say it: "There's a lot I don't know. I welcome your ideas."

Robin Bienfait, the Research In Motion CIO, talked to me about the importance of pursuing a "trust, but verify" mentality as a leader. "Within the first three years of my business career, I was asked to help manage a project with teams from across the company. How do you really know when people are only sharing the good news and not the total picture? That they really spoke to all of the customers? That they really did testing? It's a tricky balance to build a trusting team environment, without the team thinking you're second-guessing their answers," she says.

Robin says that the key to getting the full range of data, not just the good news, is creating an environment of total honesty and candor. "To do this, you have to constantly encourage open conversations in a trusting and safe environment. This feeling of security encourages the team to work more cohesively together," she says. "Everyone is focused on common goals and a sense of responsibility to report back on what is working and what needs more support from other areas of the business. When you speak on behalf of any team, set the right expectation up front about delivering both the good and bad news."

BECOME A NOVICE

As you become more senior in your career, having confidence in your knowledge and abilities isn't the constant challenge of your greener years. Your *new* challenge is to stay forever humble, patient, and curious to learn. Genevieve Bos, CEO of IdeaString, got right to the heart of it, telling me that her worst fear is to lose her sense of wonder—"to stop asking *why* and instead depend on what I already know. . . . The past or what has always worked is such an easy and tempting path—but I need to continue to foster the contrarian and knowledge seeker in me," she says. "That means I have to constantly stop going about the business of life and pay attention." You need to continue to nurture your sense of wonder and grow your knowledge base throughout your career. It's up to you to seek out the experiences that make continuous learning not just possible, but inevitable.

Dare to . . . Keep Learning

Sharpen your knowledge with the following ideas for action:

- *Pursue formal education.* Research executive educational offerings, fellowships, and conferences in your space, and petition your company to support them, either by sponsoring your tuition or by giving you paid time for learning.

- *Leverage technology.* New tools are being developed every day to help you find and process information. Social media and mobile technology mean that you have access to these tools virtually anywhere. Some of my favorite tools for knowledge gathering are Flipboard, where I aggregate my media; Engadget and TechCrunch, which I read to keep up on new mobile apps and technology; and Quora, a question-and-answer site with a vast array of highly granular, crowdsourced information.

- *Keep reading.* Are you staying on the cutting edge of information in your space? Read books, subscribe to industry publications, and follow the work of individuals who are leading change in your industry.

- *Create your own miniconferences.* Ask your employees or your peers to present information they think would be helpful for the team at a monthly or quarterly gathering. Hold your team accountable for sharing what they learn. Not everyone will be able to attend every meeting, but if those who are present take the time to share the highlights, everyone can stay informed. Make it explicitly clear that yours is a culture of learning; you know that the best information doesn't always come from the top.

- *Become a novice.* At least once a quarter, put yourself in a situation in which you are a novice. That could mean taking a course in a completely new discipline, picking up golf, or showing up in Paris prepared to practice your three months of introductory French. Recognize the rapt attention you naturally devote to those moments. Patiently observe the initial stress, and watch as it transforms into the pleasure of new mastery. Then bring that level of exploration and engagement to everything else you do.

CHAPTER SIX

DARE TO FAIL

Celebrate Failure as the Fast Track to Experience and Reward

The gem cannot be polished without friction, nor man perfected without trials.

CHINESE PROVERB

Looking back on your career to date, how many times have you failed? If your list is short, don't pat yourself on the back and assume you must be poised to jump from mid-level to executive leadership. In fact, the reality may be quite the opposite. That lack of failure suggests first and foremost that you've resisted acting with the bold daring that characterizes the most successful leaders. Instead you've spent your career avoiding risk.

If you want to move forward, it's time to get up close and personal with failure. Failure is one of the most rapid ways to develop *experience*, which is the third pillar of confidence. Degrees and programmatic learning are great, but it's experience that really qualifies you. Failure is a very specific subset of experience, one that's particularly important to gaining the skills and confidence you need to be an executive.

When we fail, we learn first and foremost that we can recover, an insight that makes it easier to act decisively going forward. When you are a leader, freezing up when faced with

111

making a decision doesn't just hurt you, it hurts every single player down the chain. You must be comfortable making decisions despite many unknowns. Serial entrepreneur and senior executive Karen Robinson Cope explains that "by learning from your early failures, you will feel more comfortable making timely decisions, even if they involve sizable risks. I learned early on that if I wasn't failing once in a while, I wasn't pushing the envelope and having the opportunity to learn from my mistakes." And it's in exactly those moments that a leader learns when to trust her gut.

Karen told me about a time in her past when failure taught her an important lesson in trusting her own her capabilities. She was the CEO of a venture-backed tech start-up that was getting ready to go public at a very high valuation with a number of well-known investment players. The stakes for this company, one that she had built from the ground up with her team—raising all of the capital and growing the customer base—were incredibly high. Despite her success up to that point, the board got nervous. They asked her to step aside to bring in a more "experienced" (*read*: male) CEO who would better appeal to Wall Street and institutional investors.

"I listened to the board and assumed they knew best, even though most of the investors and my own instincts told me otherwise," says Karen. "There were very few public companies at this time that had female CEOs." Bowing to the pressure, she yielded her position to a male CEO from a well-known Fortune 500—and then watched as things fell apart.

"It was a bad mistake that ultimately resulted in the sale of the company at a significant reduction in the sale price. Afterward, the investors and employees all said it would have been a different outcome had I remained CEO," she says. "I learned that you need to depend on your intuition, your analysis, and your personal power, even when 'conventional wisdom' says otherwise."

She went on to grow and sell her next company successfully. Two years later, her willingness to trust herself was again put to the test when she was recruited to be the CEO of an early-stage media company. Coming in, she analyzed the industry and determined that two of the three founders—both of whom, she says, "had significantly more industry experience than I did"—weren't right in their roles and would have to go. She gave the team a choice: either these two would have to resign or she would.

Both men agreed to leave. "We built the company into a very successful national media company. Five years later, we sold it to a public company, and all investors and employees made a substantial return," Karen remembers.

The experience of failure teaches us that we will survive, and even thrive, in the aftermath of a risky decision gone wrong—incredibly important, considering that those risky decisions often can lead to the biggest rewards. Diana Einterz, a telecom executive, told me that she realized this early in her career when a boss once asked her, "How often do you try to be right?" She said, "Well, usually 100 percent but surely never less than 90 percent." She was surprised when instead of congratulating her, he shook his head and told her that her track record suggested she wasn't taking enough risks.

"He was right! I was so reluctant to fail that I did not take enough risks in my career or in my projects. If I'd stretched further outside of my comfort zone, I could have achieved greater results."

One of my favorite questions to ask in job interviews was always, "Tell me about a time you failed and what you learned from it." How a candidate responded would tell me a great deal about how open this person was and how willing he or she was to seize the initiative. Only those who are content to coast, who never push the envelope, make no mistakes. Moreover, how applicants answered the question gave me insight into how innovative they were and how readily they recovered from setbacks.

For me, it was a rule of thumb: anyone interviewing for a job at the top level of an organization should be able to answer the question about failure and answer it well.

YOUR SECRET RÉSUMÉ

Every successful executive I know has what you might call a "secret résumé." They never show this "résumé" to a prospective employer, but it exists, somewhere, in the back of their mind: a private and often extensive accounting of mistakes they have made. The fact is, no one rises to the top without making mistakes or trying things and failing.

It's too bad that such secret résumés are never made public, because they reveal that failures, when handled well, aren't demerits against you. From them you take lessons that define you as a leader—lessons that are most powerfully taught in the rapid churning of experience. Looked at this way, your secret résumé is actually a stunning inventory of achievements. All of the women profiled in this book have shared personal stories of lessons learned. Stepping out of your comfort zone to overcome fear of failure or rejection is essential to acquiring the experience and insight needed to be successful. Lessons learned from failure are precisely the data that increase your odds of success on the next try—or the next after that.

My own secret résumé is plenty long. I've certainly had my share of failures.

Most of them had to do with lacking experience, not asking for help, not asking for help soon enough, or simply not doing enough homework before launching into an issue. One of my most painful failures happened early in my career. I had been given the important responsibility of creating some financial reports. These were to be shared by our CEO and CFO in a large gathering of bankers and potential investors in New York when we were in the process of raising more than $350 million of new external financing. A whole lot was riding on my assignment.

Several people had been promoted out of our department, so I was now the lead analyst in charge of the project, promoted up from grunt number cruncher. That task, my former responsibility, was assigned to a new hire who would take direction from me.

This was the early 1980s, before we had all of today's automated desktop publishing tools for quickly making beautiful, accurate spreadsheets. Our standard procedure back then was to type up all the information, insert charts into the reams of numbers as needed, then drop everything into three-ring binders. It was practical, but certainly far from sophisticated. Knowing how important it was to make an outstanding impression on the bankers and investors, I decided to take a step beyond business as usual by giving the reports a look that was more sophisticated and polished. Color graphs, formal typesetting, and permanent binding between embossed covers would, I believed, up the ante significantly. Of course, this would take hard work against an impending deadline, so I delegated the number crunching to our new person while I focused exclusively on creating the high-impact look of the reports and on coordinating the elements of the work to ensure on-time delivery.

Adding color and binding our work meant we had to work hard to meet the deadline. I devoted three eighteen-hour days to pulling together the components of this masterpiece, and, when it came back from the printer, I was extremely proud of this dazzling new way of showcasing our data. I could just imagine how thrilled the CEO and CFO were going to be with my work, and I took great pleasure in the knowledge that it was going to make *them* look very good in front of this crucially important audience.

We got everything assembled just in time for the executives to take it with them to review on the plane to New York.

What happened when they pulled the books out to review? To this day, I shudder to think of it.

They began to cross-reference the numbers in the graphs with the numbers in the text. In several places, they did not match up. At thirty-two thousand feet, my bosses realized they could not pass around the reports—not with these errors, *my* errors. Moreover, because the reports were bound, there was no way to slip in a new page with the corrected information. They had to go into the meeting, make their pitch for more money, and leave—without any hard numbers in hand to back up their case.

When my boss returned from the meeting and told me what had happened, I thought I was going to die. My anxiety and shame were through the roof. Just imagine the feeling of letting down the top people in your company precisely when you believed you had done something above and beyond, something that had taken so much personal effort.

I immediately apologized. I made no excuses. I took full responsibility for the failed reports. The look on my face spoke volumes about my devastation, and I was incredibly fortunate that the CEO and CFO were very forgiving.

I'm not going to tell you that this failure turned out to be a wonderful experience. As I write about it, I can feel those awful feelings welling up again. The fact is that the failure was terrible, entirely preventable, and absolutely my fault. The fact also is that it didn't kill me. It didn't even get me fired, and I learned a great deal from it. I still believe my out-of-the-box thinking was admirable and my objective worthy; however, what I failed to appreciate is that when you are working with someone new to a key role, you really do need to provide extra oversight. I didn't budget time for that.

The experience also made me a fanatic about fact-checking. You owe it to your team, no matter how much you trust them, to make sure their work has been thoroughly checked. It was Vladimir Lenin who first said it, but Ronald Reagan who made it famous: "Trust, but verify." I would add, *especially when you are dealing with numbers.* I learned that whenever you dare to think outside of the box—a good thing!—you must realize that you are working with new and unproven tools. That means you must also allow sufficient time to check for mistakes and to correct them. Even when a job is strictly routine, I make it a point to leave time for one final review of the work. As painful as this particular failure was, there have been many times when drawing on this bad experience has saved me a lot of anguish and my company loss of time, money, and opportunity. Not only have I made no attempt to purge the event from my memory but also to this day I keep a copy of this failed report in my desk so that I can see it every so often. Only I know the reason, of course. It serves as a great reminder of lessons

---

The Mentors Speak: On Risking Failure

Test yourself and grow by taking risks. To accelerate your learning and development, pursue opportunities and roles that seem really hard and that others don't want. Whether you succeed, fail, or end up with something in between, be tenacious.

Anesa Chaibi, president and CEO,
HD Supply Facilities Maintenance

Dive in with everything you've got; you really know more than you think you do. Learn from others around you. I have learned what to do and, more important, what *not* to do.

Hala Moddelmog, president, Arby's

I learned early to speak up as soon as I realized I made a mistake and ask for help (or forgiveness) if needed. That has worked out well for me. I think I've averted the big mistakes because I ask for help, and I work to fix problems before they get too big.

Kim Greene, president and CEO,
Southern Company Services

learned. Anytime I'm rushing to complete something important, I glance over at its embossed cover and think about how successful the report could have been with just a little more discipline, time, and due diligence. So, hurried as I am, I slow down for a double check. That is the way I've been working and managing since 1983.

Making mistakes is part of learning. Just never make the same mistake twice.

THE REAL FAILURE IN FAILURE

Failure is the common denominator of human endeavor. Written more than three centuries ago, poet Alexander Pope's line "To err is human; to forgive, divine" still rings true. Most of us pay more attention to the clause following the semicolon, but the first part is just as important. *Everyone* makes mistakes. *Everyone* fails. How this fact of human life is handled is what marks the difference between exceptionally successful people and "ordinary" ones.

The real failure is letting the fear of failure paralyze us. The mere imagining of failure and its consequences can cause us to do nothing, to accept the status quo (no matter how inadequate or miserable), and to pass up one opportunity after another because we're afraid of taking a risk.

Are women more susceptible to risk aversion? Doug Sundheim, the author of *Taking Smart Risks*, took a close look at the available data and concluded that it depends on how you define "risk." He wrote that when he was about to deliver the final manuscript of his book, he realized something he considered "disturbing": only seven of the thirty-eight smart risk takers he profiled in his book were women.[1] Looking over his process, he realized that not only had the request he sent to his network (which, by the way, was slightly weighted toward women) for potential people to profile yielded more men than women but also he had selected more of the men's stories for the book.

In looking at the available research around gender and risk, he found that most studies were focused on physical and financial risks, which men were evidently more likely than women to take. But if you were to widen the definition of *risk* to include "standing up for what's right in the face of opposition, or taking the ethical path when there's pressure to stray," Sundheim opines that women would rate much higher. He concludes that "the only way we'll redefine professional risk-taking more broadly is to identify and tell more stories of successful female risk takers, balancing the male stories that currently dominate"—an opportunity he missed in his book.

Regardless of the role of gender, if risk aversion and fear when it comes to decision making are issues for *you*, the experience of failure is one of the best ways to move beyond them. Martha McGill, chief operating officer of Miami Children's Hospital, is responsible for overseeing overall operations for the 289-bed pediatric hospital and its six ambulatory care centers. She is one of few executives operating in an environment in which everyday decision making truly does have life-or-death implications. Martha told me that her biggest career mistakes came from decision-making paralysis, "processing tough decisions for prolonged periods of time—especially when they involved significant impact on others." Then she realized the paralysis was causing more pain than the potential negative impact of the decision itself. "After toiling for months over one particularly tough decision, I finally moved forward in a direction I knew months prior I needed to go. I realized that the toll had been much harder on me and on my organization than the impact of the decision would be on others."

Fear so often prevents us from acting decisively—but how many bold actions in life do we eventually regret? A psychiatrist researching deathbed sentiments discovered that most dying people regretted very little that they had done in their lives.

Their greatest regrets—their *deathbed* regrets—concerned those things they had *not* done, those risks they had *not* taken. Maybe it sounds morbid, but I often think about this when I am presented with a new, possibly risky opportunity. I challenge myself to imagine whether I will someday lie on my deathbed, consumed with sorrow and frustration over my failure to have seized this particular opportunity. Failure never feels good. Failing to risk failure, however, feels worst of all—and typically has the worst, longest-lasting, most life-altering consequences.

TAKE A POSITIVE APPROACH TO RISK

For most of us, hardwired as we are, the challenge is to realize that life-or-death risks that require caution are not the same kinds of risks we face most of the time at work. The upside rewards of many of today's risks outweigh the downside consequences of failure. These days, it's downright healthy to evaluate a risk with the intention of taking it.

When offered an opportunity involving risk, do a gut check. Listen to your intuition. Stay positive—which means resisting a knee-jerk rejection of risk. Research the upside and the downside. Supplement your feelings with facts. Even after doing your homework, accept the fact that business decisions rarely come with a guarantee. Certainty is a scarce commodity in enterprise, these days in particular, because circumstances change so rapidly. Nevertheless, keeping up and doing your homework ahead of time not only will give you the best available information but also will minimize the amount of time you may spend heading in the wrong direction. If new information tells you you're on the wrong path, have the courage to change course—to take an alternative path in pursuit of your goal.

Taking a positive approach to risk does not mean stubbornly insisting that you are right. Stay open to new information.

If your position conflicts with someone else's, first make sure you have thoroughly harvested and rigorously winnowed the facts. Be willing to listen and get as much input as you can, but once you are convinced that you've nailed the facts, take action. Former secretary of state Colin Powell wrote, "You don't know what you can get away with until you try."[2] It's a provocative statement, but the secretary's point is not to attempt anything underhanded. It is to recognize that, sometimes, you need to take a stand against received wisdom to determine just how much you can achieve. It may very well be more than you—or anyone else—thought possible. In connection with this, Powell counsels, "Being responsible sometimes means pissing people off."[3] This can be particularly difficult for women, but we all have to accept that, if we are driving change and doing things differently, some people will see us as a threat, and they will make a fuss about it.

LEARN TO LIVE WITH FAILURE

Businesswoman Anesa Chaibi once jumped at the opportunity to helm a start-up with two other thirty-three-year-olds. They rolled up their sleeves and threw themselves at the arduous task of bootstrapping the fledgling business. But despite their capability, passion, and commitment, things fell apart when the macroeconomic environment shifted. "We missed the window to successfully enter the market. Ultimately, I ended up shutting down the business, shelving the products, and placing all of the business's top talent in other roles before I moved on to my next position," she told me.

Today, as the president and CEO of HD Supply Facilities Maintenance, a multibillion-dollar HD Supply business unit, she counts that failure as a success. "I walked away with a tremendous learning experience and the understanding that life does go on, that you have to take risks and big swings to push yourself out of your comfort zone. I have found that the benefit of pushing myself is discovering there are always things to learn from each experience (good and bad), regardless of succeeding or failing."

In fact, history brims with successful people who endured defeats before finally achieving their goals. The difference between them and those figures history judges as final failures is that the successful ones didn't give up because of a few—or even many—discouraging setbacks. Margaret Thatcher, Britain's first female prime minister and one of the most influential and powerful women of the twentieth century, was beaten the first three times she ran for office in the early 1950s. She didn't give up on her political goals, and she eventually won a seat in Parliament. In addition, during the period of her defeats, she gained great triumphs, giving birth to twins and earning a degree in tax law.

Thatcher dared to keep moving toward her goals even as she rolled over many sharp bumps in the road. If those bumps forced her into some "detours," she turned them into time spent working toward other goals that would ultimately make her a better leader. With everything she did and everything she experienced—wins or losses—she added fuel to her ambitions, and she realized her dreams in an era when women were encouraged to stay out of the professional world. Yes, she accepted defeat, but she never accepted it as final. The result was history-making success.

Thomas Alva Edison may be the most prolific inventor in history, with 1,093 U.S. patents to his name, including one of the most successful inventions of all time—the lightbulb. He was also famously prolific in his failures, seeing them not as shameful or a waste of time, but rather as part of the process. "None of my inventions came by accident. I see a worthwhile need to be met and I make trial after trial until it comes," he said at a 1929 press conference. "What it boils down to is one per cent inspiration and ninety-nine per cent perspiration."[4]

Follow the example of Edison and other breakthrough thinkers. Do your thoughtful up-front analysis, but if, having done that, you still fail, learn from it. Examine it. Pry open the lessons it has to offer, and use them to inform your next step. If it teaches you something, it is not a failure.

This rapid learning process is one reason why it is so important to take on stretch assignments—the kind that carry a significant risk of failing. Another reason stretch roles are so important is that, as psychologist Peter Buckley of Georgia Regents University told me, "experience is essential to building a confident attitude."[5] Stretch assignments bring on those moments when you learn that "what doesn't kill you makes you stronger," according to Peter. "Even if you fail, the experience of those stretch assignments provides the lessons to help you be successful on the next try."

Rebecca Jacoby echoed that exactly when telling me about a time she and a team were given an assignment judged so ridiculous that for the first two months, the project team just sat around talking about how impossible it was. "We had a fairly wise leader who allowed us to vent, and then one day he came into our meeting room and told us the time for venting was over. He said we were to get the assignment done or they would find someone else to do it. After realizing we wasted two months and only had ten months to finish, we put forth the effort and achieved our goal within seven months. Once you have the experience of accomplishing something like this, you no longer believe anything is impossible."

When you don't manage to accomplish your stretch assignment successfully, or when you make mistakes along the way, generally speaking, people will forgive you. What they have a hard time forgiving is seeing you make the same mistake over and over again. That's why after admitting a mistake, the most important thing you can do is present what you will do differently (and better!) next time. And then do it!

In fact, a history of overcoming challenges and failures—and owning them—can make you an even more compelling role model for others. Take Oprah Winfrey. When we think about Oprah Winfrey and the vast media empire she has created, we think *success.* She is among the most powerful, admired, and all-around successful women in history. Yet the backstory, we now know, is one of childhood poverty—first in rural Mississippi and then in Milwaukee's tough inner city—rape at nine, and pregnancy at fourteen (her son died in infancy). As an adult, she landed a job in radio, then managed to get on television as a reporter—only to be fired as "unfit for TV."

This could be called *failure.* She called it *experience,* and didn't let it discourage her. She went on to prove herself by the numbers, lifting a local Chicago TV talk show from the ratings cellar to the top spot in the market, beating out the number one Chicago talk show, *Donahue.* Today, the woman once declared unfit for television now owns her own television network.

THE FIVE MOST POWERFUL WORDS

Even after more than three decades in a business career—just when I think I've seen everything—I find myself still amazed at the pretzel-like contortions people will tie themselves into just to cover up having made a mistake. Even on the little things, some folks will go to extraordinary lengths to erase culpability. People just hate to be wrong, and they are willing to take enormous risks—the *wrong* kind of risks, dead-end risks with no upside—to cover their tracks. Remember the lesson of the Watergate scandal: "It's not the crime, it's the cover-up that gets you."

What defines you as a leader is how you take ownership of your flubs and flops, and, having done this, how you go on to manage them. It isn't the failure that defines us. It's the recovery. Universally, people who accept responsibility for mistakes command greater respect and influence. When asked, clients will tell you that their most trusted contractors and vendors have not been perfect, but when a mistake was made, they admitted it and took immediate steps not only to correct it but also to make it right—typically through a discount, a replacement, or some other extra-mile consideration. Taking ownership of a failure, a mistake, doesn't just mean accepting blame; it means accepting the responsibility to make things right. The upside of this, for you, is that the combination of graciously and courageously accepting blame *and* working toward a remedy often actually *adds* value to your brand.

The most powerful thing you can do when you make a mistake or otherwise fail is to embrace responsibility—and to do so quickly. It's hard for someone to hurl stones at you and misinterpret what happened when you step up to own the problem. This does not mean that you should allow yourself to be thrown under the bus for something in which you had no involvement. But if you are even 10 percent involved, you have an incredible opportunity to build trust by sharing responsibility.

Start with five very powerful words: "I'm sorry, please forgive me."

I have diffused many difficult situations with these very words. They're simple enough, of course, yet, for some people, they stick in the throat. Instead of uttering them, some of us bury ourselves in the blame game. Not only does this make us look bad (nobody likes a buck passer) but also it creates ill will among everyone involved in the problem at issue, and it gets in the way of realizing the benefit the failure offers: the opportunity to learn.

In addition to creating a climate of forgiveness by dispelling anger and repairing trust, the five words make it possible for you and others to begin to focus on solutions. Apologize sincerely, and suddenly people stop devoting time and energy

The Limits of Contrition

We've all seen it—a sports hero, a rising politician, or a business leader caught having committed some gross ethical violation or maybe even a crime appears before the TV cameras to "come clean." And he or she *does* make an admission and deliver an apology. But rarely is it an admission of actual wrongdoing. Instead, choking back tears (genuine or simulated), the sad figure on-screen confesses to having "made a mistake."

Deceiving a colleague, cheating a customer, betraying a confidence, lying to government regulators, cooking the books—such acts may be ethical violations, crimes, or something in between, but they are emphatically *not* "mistakes." The one risk you should never take—you cannot afford to take—is to cut ethical or legal corners. Depending on the magnitude of the wrongdoing, it may or may not be the end of your career. There may well be a way to make things right again; however, any action that violates trust damages your reputation for integrity.

to finger-pointing and instead start actually solving problems. They may reach out and embrace you, and they may even admit part of the fault as their own. You build and enhance trust by holding yourself accountable and accepting personal responsibility.

Once, I learned that one of our executives was very upset with my team after we came in way under our target budget for his organization. Because we were under budget, his team missed an opportunity to spend dollars on other items that they needed. After hearing from one of my reports that he was upset, I immediately took the initiative and called to set up a face-to-face meeting with him and our respective teams. In preparation, I met with my team to discuss the issue. The members were understandably defensive and eager to assign the blame to the executive's team. In fact, they had a good point. After all, it was *his* team that had negotiated a delivery date on some products that failed to arrive in time to hit *our* year-end budget. Arguably, this is what had put us under budget.

It was very tempting to point the finger back at the other guy, especially because there were reasonable grounds for doing just that. Nevertheless, I stressed to my team that we would not use this approach. Instead, regardless of the circumstances, we would listen to his concerns, we would take ownership of the issue, and *I* would apologize. We would then begin a discussion about how our teams could work better together in the future to ensure this did not happen again. The people on my team were not at all happy with this direction, but they agreed to support it.

As the main meeting began, the executive's irritation was painfully obvious. We let him vent, and then I apologized for what had happened: "I'm sorry. Please forgive me." I told him we were aware of the situation we had placed him in, and we wanted to put a plan in place to prevent it from happening in the future.

His irritation turned to shock. He was simply stunned that we had accepted responsibility for the issue. As soon as he could speak, he admitted that some of the problem had been the product of poor communication from *his* team. From this moment on, he was wide open to talking about what we could do together to improve the process in the future. In a moment, his whole attitude toward us had changed. Those five little words got us back on track with this important ally. Our willingness to accept responsibility for the mistake and come up with a plan to move forward together both averted repetition of the problem and created a stronger, more cooperative dynamic within our company.

When Benjamin Franklin said that only two things were certain, death and taxes, he could well have added a third and a fourth: error and failure. It's not a question of *if* these things will occur, it's *when*; and when they happen, using the five words— "I'm sorry, please forgive me"—will put you and the others involved in position to fail forward, faster. Because failure is a fact of life, it is best to get on with learning from your lapse to keep progressing in a positive way. Why wallow in blame?

Part of failing forward faster is recognizing when you've made a mistake and being ready to change course quickly to get back on track. Develop solutions for how you'll approach things differently without dwelling on the fact of failure. Although you should take the time necessary to discover the sources of the failure, take action as soon as possible. Sometimes you even have to have the courage to back up a few steps, admit your error, and start over. Failing forward may require stepping backward before you can regain your forward momentum.

CREATE A FORGIVING ENVIRONMENT

In high-performing businesses, we often speak about creating a demanding environment, an environment of high expectations. That is important, but, when you become a leader, your goal should be to create a demanding environment that is also a forgiving environment. This is particularly true on a senior leadership team, because the model will cascade down into every level of the organization. If people are afraid to make mistakes, afraid to fail, they will never stretch, and that means that they—as well as your organization—will be doomed to the mediocrity of the status quo. An uncompetitive business does not survive, let alone excel. You need to be vigilant about creating and maintaining the kind of forgiving environment that promotes risk taking and, therefore, heightens achievement.

Healthy competition in the workplace can be a highly productive force, unless the emphasis on winning turns the environment into a zero-sum game—a scenario in which, for you to "win," someone else must lose. The idea, of course, is for the department, the team, the company to win. Avoid the zero-sum trap by never purposely embarrassing anybody. Do whatever it takes to have the bigger character and not publicly humiliate anyone. There's a time and place for everything, even the kind of frank communication that tells someone he or she has made a mistake. Don't be so much in a hurry to be right about something that you forget that being "right" isn't your job in the moment. Your job is to help someone else learn something.

I moderated a panel with some of the most successful women in corporate America. One of our key takeaways was, "Just because you think you're right, doesn't mean you are." What the panelist who said this meant was that even if you have "correct" information, your audience will perceive you as wrong if you impart it by hurting others or if you broadcast it at the wrong time or place or in some way that is perceived as wrong.

When you challenge the thoughts of others, do it in a professional way. If the information you possess has the potential to embarrass someone, convey the material in private. By doing so, you will find that you've made an ally instead of creating an enemy. Intimidate others, however, and you will be likely to find yourself isolated. You will be seen as a person bent on making herself look good at others' expense. Without allies, you're lost. If you disagree with what is being said, ask questions, ask for advice, and ask for explanations—and do so in a respectful way. Do it in person, and not in an e-mail. This approach will make others feel valued and help you establish trust. It is by building a workplace ethos that demands the very best yet forgives failure and error that you make a space for yourself and for others to stretch, to think outside the box, to take creative risks, and to rise.

GAME ON, NOT GAME OVER

Huge wins can come from having the courage to fail—and that means having the imagination to think of failure not as final, an end, but as a step toward success. Many great careers have recovered from failure, have restarted from failure, and have even begun with failure.

Anna Maria Chávez, CEO of Girl Scouts of the USA, told me that the founder, Juliette Gordon Low, searched for many years of her life for the best way to channel her desire to make a difference, without finding her way. It wasn't until she was in her fifties that she came across the then-nascent concept of scouting. "Winston Churchill once said that success is going from failure to failure without loss of enthusiasm. The operative word is *enthusiasm*, right?" says Anna. "Low threw herself at the task with an incredible energy and enthusiasm, and changed the world."

If you want to rise to the top jobs in corporate America, recast disaster as an opportunity to do better. Embrace the lessons, the responsibility, and the personal growth that will come out of the experience, preparing you for newer and bigger challenges in the next round.

Failure isn't game over. It's *game on.*

Dare to . . . Know the Dos and Don'ts of Failure

Do . . .

- Acknowledge the mistake as quickly as you can and apologize if needed
- Learn from the mistake
- Plan what you will do differently next time
- Propose a plan to make things right
- Draw on the experience and help of others
- Share the failure so others can learn from it
- Get back out there

Don't . . .

- Be defensive
- Point a finger or pass the buck
- Make long-winded excuses
- Stop trying
- Stop experimenting

CHAPTER SEVEN

DARE TO REACH OUT

Build a Support Network of Allies, Mentors, and Sponsors

It is a fact that in the right formation, the lifting power of many wings can achieve twice the distance of any bird flying alone.

UNKNOWN

People used to say to me something to the effect of, "You've been on a rocket to the top of the corporate world!" When they did, I would thank them for their kind remark, but then think to myself: "It sure didn't *feel* that way!"

I spent a dozen years in the beginning stages of my career in accounting and finance, which, believe me, sometimes felt like a lifetime. But that experience, unglamorous though it was, helped me build the solid foundation that's required for liftoff. Some of that foundation comprised experience and knowledge, but equally as important was the broad, company-wide network of trusting human relationships I had the opportunity to build in those years.

Although it is you who must take ultimate responsibility for your career, business leadership can never be, by simple definition, a solo act. It is other people who give you the strength and support that help you grow as a professional. The more people you have relationships with, the more access you will have to knowledge and opportunities.

131

Once you reach a certain level, you will find that most of
your peers are competent managers. After all, it takes an ability
to deliver on goals and a certain amount of experience to
get promoted into middle management. What will launch you
into higher career levels beyond competence is your ability to
develop and leverage relationships. The capacity and will to
reach out and work with others will position you to climb to the
top rungs of the corporate ladder.

Employees have often come to me for advice on how to
build a network. Just about everyone thinks this is important,
yet few people can figure out how to get started. Building
an incredible network is about daring to be more than your job
title or your current company, and daring to see others in the
same light; daring to reach out beyond your immediate circle to
build a network that follows you wherever you go.

The search for allies, mentors, and sponsors should have
you stepping outside of your company or your current team.
From the very beginning of your career, your goal should be to
build a network of both personal and professional contacts who
are connected to *you*, specifically, not just you in whatever your
current role is.

Right now, when somebody asks whom you do business with,
chances are you respond by reeling off a list of companies and
corporations.

Stop doing that.

People never do business with companies, they do business
with people. Stop looking for companies. Start looking for
people you can reach out to for help in making your individual
professional foundation solid.

Never forget that personal relationships—your family
and friends—are at the heart of everything you do, and
how you manage them either empties or fills the well of
energy you have for your professional life. I also often hear
from people who ask for my guidance on networking, "I'd
network more, but then I'd never be at home." That's why this

chapter about network building kicks off with a discussion of family.

PUT YOUR FAMILY FIRST WITHOUT PUTTING YOUR JOB LAST

A woman in the corporate world might feel like she is precariously spinning plates while balancing eggs on her head. We women handle a lot—every day. Betty Siegel, whom you met earlier, was the first woman to lead a public university in the state of Georgia and did so for twenty-five years, making her the longest-serving female president of a state university in the nation. She was and is also a wife, a mother, a writer, and a mentor to many.

"You can call it spinning plates or juggling balls," she says. "We all have lots of things to keep in motion. I think of the balls I juggle this way: some are made of rubber, and if they fall, they bounce and it's okay. Some of them are made out of crystal, and if they fall, they will shatter. You can't easily repair those, so what you don't want to do is drop the crystal ones. The crystal ones represent your family, your friends, and your health. The rubber ones are work." Surround yourself with a network of talent, and you will ensure that you will never drop the balls of crystal at home and that somebody will always be there to help you catch those rubber balls at work, if not on the fly, at least on the rebound, before they really get away from you.

The rubber balls represent things you can delegate at work and even at home. The things that you *cannot* delegate are taking care of yourself and being there for your loved ones. Many elements go into what we define as success in our lives. You cannot be successful in life if you become the CEO but have neglected or ignored the other important aspects of your life, especially friends and family. "Family" includes your family of origin, your spouse's or partner's family, your spouse, your children, and your pets.

Many women fear that a career in the C-suite is tantamount to willful child neglect. No female corporate leader will tell you that getting the balance right is easy. But speaking as a former executive whose husband also had a demanding career, and as the mother of a successful daughter, I can tell you that it can be done. And at the time I was, as far as I know, the only woman in the neighborhood who worked.

Lora G. Weiss, lab chief scientist at Georgia Tech Research Institute, described to me the challenge of the "two-body" problem as follows:

> There is a saying in the scientific community that "the two-body problem is harder to solve than the three-body problem." In physics, the *three-body problem* is one that requires determining all the possible motions of three bodies, such as planets or stars, moving under the force of gravity. After more than a century, it remains unsolved. Physicists have no trouble solving the two-body problem—unless those two bodies are a successful husband and a successful wife trying to find jobs in the same city without either making a career compromise. Balancing career aspirations of two highly talented individuals takes significant courage.

Lora and her husband have both made compromises in their own respective careers to ensure their partner's success, and it has worked for them and for their two children. She says that having a supportive partner has helped provide the courage and confidence to excel in their careers at a pace that also meets their family's needs. Still, she says that balancing work responsibilities with the needs of her family is an ongoing, daily struggle—but one that she is willing to manage. "We have had many close calls, as one of us is heading to the airport while the other is returning home from the airport, but we've always been able to ensure that one parent is home while the other is out of town," she says. "The question of who put their trip on the calendar first has become our family joke."

Whether you've got a partnership like the one Lora describes or if you're flying solo, it's a great idea to throw away the narrow, rigid idea of the nuclear family when it comes to conceiving of a support system for your home life. Don't make the high-powered careerist's frequent mistake of skimping on friendships.

The truest friends share both your good times and your tough times. If you nurture these relationships, your life will be enriched immeasurably, and it will be made much easier, too. Good friends will cover for you when you need them to, as you would (and must) for them. Friendship is, of course, a two-way street. When it comes time for you to make deposits in the International Bank of Karma, make them generously. Maintain a hefty balance in that human capital account, and then you can make withdrawals when you really need to.

Moreover, at whatever point you are in your life or your career, it's never too late to make a new friend. People are put into your life for a reason, and don't dismiss someone as useless or too different from you to be a friend. Your job, when new people come along, is to figure out why they are there, what you can learn from them, how they can help you grow, and how you can enhance their lives.

If you have children, your kids themselves are an important factor in the question of how to manage your home life. Don't try to guess what's important to them, just ask them. *Interview* your kids. Ask them directly, "What's important to you? What really matters to you?" Ask what they want you to do for them. "What can I help you with?" "What can I do better for you?" "What events do you want me to attend?"

I got the advice about "interviewing" my daughter early in my career. It proved to be a simple but great lesson. Early on, I felt very guilty that I was unable to take my daughter to and from school each day. I talked to her about it, and I asked her what really mattered *to her*. As it turned out, she really didn't care about my not being able to drive her. What *was* important to her was for me to be there when it was my time to read to her class. You can bet this became a top priority for me. It was the most important task I had, and I put lots of effort into the book I selected and how I interacted with her class.

The Mentors Speak: On Reaching Out

Developing the necessary relationships [for success] can be a challenge, particularly if you are juggling work, family, *and* taking care of yourself. It is easy to see why there is so little time for a lunch or a drink after work, much less attending a business-sponsored event, such as an exhibit opening. In fact, you do *not* have to lunch every day or attend every event, but you do need to choose the occasions that work best for you and then be sure to use them wisely. Don't stand in the corner. Talk to people!

Molly B. Burke, *former general counsel,*
GE Energy Services

In my TV career, I moved from a production assistant, to writer, to producer, to reporter, to news anchor by working hard, focusing on the details, and being grateful for the team that helped me do my job every day. Being collegial and generous goes a long way toward building your network, recruiting allies, and helping you succeed. Also, don't be afraid to ask for help. When you get help or advice, you also recruit an investor. That person now has some skin in the game and will do all they can to ensure your success.

Kathleen Matthews, *chief communications*
and public affairs officer, Marriott International

Seek out the wisest, most experienced person in your field and ask them to mentor you. You will be surprised at how many very accomplished, highly experienced leaders are honored to help.

Martha McGill, *COO, Miami Children's Hospital*

Martha McGill, chief operating officer at Miami Children's Hospital, offered another great piece of advice. "With work, there will always be deadlines and commitments. This is true with family as well," she said. "I've learned to schedule my family time a year in advance (yes, a year!). This approach ensures that I can fit the work around my family, which is top on the priority list."

Kids don't really ask for the moon. In fact, you will be surprised by how focused and reasonable their requests are. We all know successful women who tell us they regret missing out on things—events, moments—that they found out were very important to their kids only long after the fact. Don't let that happen to you. Be nice to your kids. They'll be the ones who pick out your nursing home someday.

FINDING COLLEAGUES—AT OTHER COMPANIES

I can tell you this quite frankly: my network of peers and other business relationships *outside the company* has at times spelled the difference between triumph and disaster when I have encountered problems as well as opportunities I did not believe I could handle on my own.

Once you are in any senior role, you'll look in vain for a textbook to tell you how to address all of the challenges. Even if it were possible to write one, such a resource would be obsolete before it was completed, let alone published. Nowhere is this truer than in fields that are technology and information intensive. In these areas, change is fast and dramatic. Newer, better, faster tools are being created each day. And newer, thornier problems emerge right along with each advance. You can't just pass off problems to someone down the chain; you've got to draw on whatever resources you can muster, and relationships with peers are often the very best.

A peer relationship rescued me from the biggest catastrophe I ever experienced during my tenure as a CIO. One summer, we had an intern in IT. One of the simple jobs we gave him was sweeping the servers to remove data before turning them in when they went off lease. It's a pretty easy thing to do: you just use a big magnet to wipe them clean of data. There is, however, an important first step, and we failed to train him to do it. Before wiping the data, the server must be unplugged from the network. Uninformed, the intern didn't do this. Instead, he went in, started sweeping, and kicked off a failure that cascaded throughout our entire network. His action randomly deleted about 20 percent of the company's data and impaired our ability to issue payroll to twenty-six thousand employees.

This was a CIO's worst nightmare. I immediately mobilized a team to restore the missing data. About eight hours into the operation, we had recovered a significant portion of the loss, but we just couldn't get it all. Of course, I wanted it all. We needed it all. No manual, no textbook, nothing in my experience gave me a clue how to get the data back. That's when I reached out to an IT peer at another company, a good friend of mine. I rang her up and explained the situation, ending by admitting: "I just don't know what else to do."

"I've been there," she responded. "This happened to us."

I cannot tell you how welcome those words were.

Her company had recently outsourced some of its work, and the outsourcer had unintentionally wiped out a significant amount of company data.

"Your problem is that you don't have enough storage," she explained with a certainty born of firsthand experience. "You've got to get on the phone right now and get some additional storage because you'll never get all the outstanding data back with the amount you have. It's a huge data surge on the same network. Look, let me call my supplier right now to help you out."

This conversation took place at about six o'clock on the evening of the day on which the wipe occurred. Called by my friend, the supplier swung into action immediately. The type of equipment we needed was not just sitting on a store shelf. He had to pull equipment out of another company's facility, and then he trucked it in to us in the middle of the night. As for me, I spent the night in the building, and by morning, all the remaining data started coming back.

My friend provided me with great advice. Her supplier in turn came through like a champ. Having the peer relationship in place—and her having a great supplier relationship to rely on—allowed me to turn the crisis around. I say "allowed me," but the takeaway is that I could not have done it without the help of my peer, my talented team, and the supplier. It was a powerful lesson in the crucial importance of building and maintaining a network—of understanding that you work with people, not with a "corporate entity." If I had had to manage the crisis alone, we would have suffered data loss—at what cost to the company and to me, I don't even want to guess.

Although each company has its own unique culture and environment, business organizations are much more alike than most of us realize. As long as your company and another are not direct competitors, you should create strong relationships with your counterparts at other companies. This is a great way to gain general knowledge and specific ideas about improving your own organization and solving problems. Why reinvent the wheel? No one in my organization, including me, had been through anything like our data loss before, and no one at my company knew what to do about it. My counterpart at the other company had the experience and had the answer. It had, incidentally, taken her *three* days to figure out how to fix her own situation, but because she now knew just what to tell me, I was able to fix the problem overnight.

Don't strand yourself on an island. Reach out to build strong relationships with smart peers, use their input to build

---

Seek Supplier Insights

You come to rely on your ability to stay on the cutting edge. You come to rely on your network of peers, who can teach you so much—especially those who have already been down a particular path, tried out a new tool, or changed a process. Don't forget suppliers as a resource. They can offer a wealth of information about systems and tools to run your organization more effectively. Whenever I've taken a new job or moved into a new position, I have always been eager to meet the top suppliers. They offer great insight into how well your organization is running compared to other companies they support. Of course, you do need to bear in mind that suppliers are also always trying to sell you something, but the best ones understand that they won't long have your business if they sell you something you don't actually need.

---

better systems, and have their information handy in case outright disaster strikes. Just as important, they can call on you. Successful business relationships only work if they are two-way streets. You have to be there for your peers as much as you expect them to be available for you. You will rapidly discover that giving help is just as valuable as getting it. Aiding a colleague in need broadcasts your integrity, authority, and expertise throughout a company and even an entire industry.

BUILDING THE NETWORK

Building a web of external relationships takes time. Start by trying to identify five individuals who do what you do and would be good people to exchange information with. They might be peers in your industry or in another field who share your title or something similar. If your network isn't very well developed, finding those five and cultivating a relationship may not prove to be as easy as it seems. You may have to make the effort to seek them out, which means attending functions and events that build your network. I'm often told by women, particularly those with children, that they don't have time for these activities. What they are really communicating is that they don't think these events are important enough to prioritize.

Here they are wrong. External relationships can be valuable in helping you get your job done effectively (or at all), but they are even more important when it comes to your professional advancement. Because there are many capable people competing for each great opportunity, connections often determine the outcome. A connection can be a relationship with someone who does no more than float your name when it might not otherwise have been thought of, or a relationship with the decision maker who gets you the job or helps you close a sale. You don't have to go to every event—but you do need to go to some, so find the best opportunities and then squeeze as much advantage as you can out of them.

You can jump-start external relationships by reaching out through a trade association relevant to your business and your field, and attending the association's events. Another good start can be made by volunteering for company-sponsored community and charity events. Whereas trade association events will introduce you to your counterparts in other companies, a company-sponsored event will get you acquainted with others across your own organization. This is a great way to learn new things about your company. If the event is big enough to include other firms, so much the better. Reach out to your counterparts, arrange a meeting, and ask for a tour of their company facilities. People love to talk about what they do, and they appreciate others' showing interest in their work.

Not all networking needs to start "in real life." Social media provides a wide-ranging means of connecting to others. I encourage you to leverage social media to initiate introductions. Do be aware, however, that at some point online relationships need to be nurtured face-to-face. Don't make the mistake of thinking that digital technology can replace human interaction. It can get a relationship launched, but it is up to you to move that relationship to the next stage, and to do so in person.

One of the most effective networkers I know is Ricky Steele, a fellow Atlantan and a great friend. He has written a firsthand account of his professional life as a networker, called *The Heart of Networking*, and he frequently speaks on the subject of building effective networks. He says that your networking strategy for events should begin long before you arrive. You need to do some research on the organization behind the event and on just who will be attending. Next, narrow your focus—and your research—to the attendees you most want to connect with. When the day comes, make it a point to arrive early to the meeting. Mosey over to the table where the name badges are laid out. Look them over. They are not state secrets. Get an idea of who is actually attending the event, and make mental notes of whom you'd like to meet that day.

You may find it difficult, but Ricky advises that you be forward in introducing yourself to others. Positive, affirmative, open body language is important. Deliver a firm handshake—I still shake hands all the time with women whose limp grasp seems to murmur, "I can't, I'll break." Make the ensuing conversation about the other person, and look him or her in the eye. Ricky's premise is that if you can find a way to help the other person, you can begin to build a sustainable relationship. If you can build the relationship, then business is likely to follow.

When you meet a new person, you want to stand out, to differentiate yourself as a leader. One way to do this from the very first meeting is to deliver a memorable message, and the best way to deliver it is to listen. Ask questions. Understand the other person's interests and concerns. Create your own message in direct response to them. Nothing is better remembered or more valued than communication that speaks directly to another's needs and wants.

Once you have met your five new "colleagues" and have initiated other new relationships, you're not finished. You've just begun. You must go on to devote the necessary effort to following up with notes or calls to arrange the next meeting. Building a network should not be left to chance any more than building a house. Plan and work, work, work, with skill and a commitment to achieve excellent results. When you do have those five peers in your network, keep building the relationships. Meet with them regularly. Share best practices and other personal and professional experiences. Share anecdotes about business, career, and life challenges you've faced and conquered.

Your first goal should always be to build *others'* trust in *you*. You must develop your personal brand as one of absolute integrity. It is a brand others can and will buy into. A reputation for integrity will help you recruit the people you need to advance. That's why it is always so important to follow up when you say you will, and to do what you committed to do. When a relationship is new, even small gestures matter. Following through is your first opportunity to show them the quality of your character. If you slip up, you may not get another chance.

We often talk about "climbing the corporate ladder." In fact, what you really climb is a corporate *net*. You succeed, you rise to leadership, by building a network. But the thing is, you cannot build a network by focusing on yourself. The network you build must be of value to others, to everyone in "your" network, if you want to benefit from it yourself.

MENTORS KEEP YOU MOVING FORWARD

Every woman I interviewed mentioned the importance of finding mentors, and shared helpful advice that had been given to them by mentors, both male and female. Indeed, almost every pivotal career moment I have included in this book features me turning to a mentor for advice.

Mentors are vital for coaching you through a risky assignment or tough challenge. They are naturally less emotionally invested in the situation than you are, and they have the experience to provide you with relevant perspectives, evidence, explanations, novel solutions, and negotiating techniques that may not have occurred to you. Obviously, most of these needs can be met by either men or women—really, anyone whom you respect and who wants to contribute to your development.

The McKinsey study referenced in Chapter One found that "structural obstacles" were also among the things that women perceived as causing them to drop out of a corporate career.[1] Foremost among the obstacles identified were "lack of access to informal networks where [women] can make important connections, a lack of female role models higher up in the organization, and a lack of sponsors to provide opportunities, which many male colleagues have."

Corporate culture has long offered men many opportunities for informal mentoring. Career-building conversations started in the boss's office are often continued on the golf course, at the gym, or even in the men's room. Over the years, more formal mentoring programs also developed, but often they were still dominated by a male-centered corporate culture.

One of the most sobering conversations I had as I interviewed women for this book was with Roberta Bondar, whom you met in Chapter One. Roberta is one of the most accomplished women I have ever met. She was the first Canadian woman and also the first neurologist to travel into space. She told me about her first experience with gender bias and times later in life when it impacted her ability to learn and develop. Her first experience occurred in eighth grade when Roberta became a school crossing guard. The process required taking a safety test, which bestowed the title of Captain upon the student who scored highest. As test results were announced, the Headmaster recognized Roberta for achieving the coveted top score. However, because Roberta was a girl, she could not be Captain. The Headmaster told her that girls only served as Lieutenant, not as Captain. Roberta was stunned and so were her parents, who protested the school's bias. In the end, a boy remained Captain.

Over the years she had many more challenges like this, but they were more subtle. Nonetheless, they were all numbing experiences. She said, "They are things that happen to you and you know it is because you are a woman. For instance, when I was a resident in neurology, I changed and washed up for surgery in a room with women, who were mostly nurses. At the same time, my male counterparts would be washing up with senior surgeons and discussing cases of the day. I would miss out on this discussion, which was a very important part of the learning process." Roberta continued, "I have worked with many men who had a hard time relating to a woman on a level that was not social. I have not been included in dinners because I was not married. Single men were included, but not me. These dinners extended conversation about medical cases, and were a missed learning opportunity for me." While these are examples from the medical world, this same type of activity occurs in the business world. Gender bias spans *all* professional industries. One of the best ways to overcome this bias is through formal and informal mentoring processes. Fortunately, companies have been putting in place mentoring programs, some especially for women and others focusing equally on women and men. Many of today's top companies assign new employees a mentor (or "buddy") when they first begin work. And although women continue to be very significantly underrepresented at the top, the number of female C-level executives is slowly growing. With this growth, the opportunities for informal mentoring for rising women have increased.

If you've felt that the men in your organization are unavailable to you as mentors or sponsors, or if you've felt shut out of those "informal" networks, ask yourself whether you've really put these assumptions to the test. If you haven't, you may just need to approach the situation with a little more daring.

When I was at the middle-management level and was being considered for my first officer role, I got passed over. After this happened, I approached my boss to discuss any feedback he may have received. He told me I would probably need to make a couple of lateral moves before I would be able to move to the next level. I reminded him that my last two career moves and the position I currently held had been lateral moves, and I wondered how many *more* I would be expected to make. Then I summoned all my courage, and very calmly confronted him with the fact that I did not have the same access to networking and information as my male peers. At the time, I was the only woman who reported to him.

He was dumbfounded, so I gave him several examples. I told him I had worked on his team for over four years and he had never once asked me to lunch. His response was, "I never go to lunch with my direct reports."

I wouldn't let him off the hook. "I park next to you," I said, "and I am always seeing you go to lunch with my peers, and you play golf and hunt with them, too. Also, two weeks ago you, the CEO, and several other male officers, as well as one of my peers, traveled together to visit a military customer. You toured a submarine, went hunting, and were together for over four days. Who do you think knows more about what is happening in our company? That peer or me?"

My boss was stunned. I had very calmly, but firmly and clearly, helped him see something he was totally unaware of. I sincerely do not think it ever occurred to him that I was being left out. To his credit, he listened to what I had to say, and he responded: "You know, you have a point." Even better, he called the next week to invite me to lunch, and he thanked me for my candor. From that point on, he began to make it a point to include me in more of the social aspects of our business.

My frank response could have backfired on me. But I protected myself by making my case firmly but also calmly, in a respectful manner that relied not on subjective feelings, but on facts bolstered by examples. And for his part, my boss responded professionally and without defensiveness.

People will mentor you, but sometimes you have to teach them how. Many times we get excluded from networking because those who do the excluding are simply unaware of it. We must dare to help them see the light.

Based on my own years in corporate America, I do suggest that female executives today find at least one mentor who is female—especially those who are still working in leadership teams that are mostly male. It can be very lonely when you're in the minority, and other women are uniquely familiar with the challenges this presents. Although we have advanced significantly in making the workplace more welcoming to both genders, women and men still face very different challenges as they navigate the exacting pressures and demands of leadership. The higher you rise, the more closely people will scrutinize you. Yet, despite the scrutiny, there may be times when the men don't hear your voice, or filter it through their assumptions about your "femininity." These moments may be subtle rather than overt, but in my experience, they will present themselves. You already know that taking risks is essential to success. It is also true that taking risks can be scary—in any situation. The fear of failure, however, is compounded when you feel both watched and marginalized—especially if you don't have support.

WHOM SHOULD YOU RECRUIT AS A MENTOR?

Mentors are critically important to women aspiring to the male-dominated C-suite. You cannot afford to wait for someone to create a formal corporate mentoring program. Find a mentor. In fact, find more than one. Start creating your own inner circle of mentors. Think of it as your personal board of directors.

Mentors are easier to find and to recruit than you may at first think. People are surprisingly eager to share their wisdom with you. If you are like many, you are shy about asking for help, but the fact is that most experienced people love to share. Sharing is satisfying, and it makes them feel valued. Studies have shown that people underestimate by as much as 50 percent the likelihood that others will agree to a direct request for help or assistance.[2] So find yourself a good mentor, somebody you can both trust and learn from and who, you believe, is in a position to advocate productively on your behalf. Usually, people of this caliber have many individuals knocking down their door, so prepare to make yourself stand out. You have to become someone a mentor will want to invest his or her time and energy—someone who radiates promise.

Mentors can be found all around you. Seek someone you truly respect, a person who has the kind of life and work you'd like to have. You don't have to come right out and ask your target candidate to be your mentor. Ease into it by asking for advice or input on a single specific topic. Evaluate the results. If you are pleased, cultivate the relationship by asking about more.

Remember, mentoring can take various forms. Maybe it's the occasional lunch or phone conversation, or regular e-mail exchange. Technology has created lots of new tools for getting mentoring and advice online. I always encourage people to use these tools; however, it is easier to develop your mentor into a sponsor (a role we'll discuss in just a moment) when you receive mentoring face-to-face. It's up to you to drive the relationship— no senior-level person is ever going to chase you down to help you out. Take the initiative to set meetings and make sure they are productive by sharing an agenda in advance. If that sounds more "take charge" than you're comfortable with, take it from me that your mentor will be grateful for this clear guide to what you'd like to glean from your interaction. It may be the one meeting that day at which he or she *doesn't* have to drive the agenda.

As with any other meaningful and valuable relationship, don't let this one become a one-way street. Show your gratitude. At the simplest level, this means saying thanks. It also means supplying feedback. Report on your progress. If your mentor suggests a solution to a problem and you implement that solution, tell him or her how it turned out. Above all, let your mentor know how his or her counsel has helped you. Proactively ask your mentor how you can help him or her, and, hey, why don't *you* buy the lunch once in a while?

The most obvious candidates for mentoring you are people in your firm who already do the job you would like to do. However, according to Helene Lollis, president of a leadership development consultancy called Pathfinders, the best mentor-mentee relationships aren't necessarily between two people in the same function or career track. "I've never met a woman in finance who didn't tell me that her mentor *had* to be in finance, because no one else could understand the unique pressures," says Helene. "But after interviewing, we may find that effective interpersonal communication skills are what she really needs to get to the next level, being able to bring a story to the numbers. So what she probably needs is a mentor specialized in communications, a place she would have never thought to look."

You don't need to limit your pool of potential mentors to your company. One very good reason for joining your college alumni association and keeping up with fellow members is that this group forms a natural resource for mentoring. In addition, professional or industry organizations are likely resources, and these days you can also log into LinkedIn to identify potential mentors.

One source of mentors that is easily overlooked is people *below* your level. No law says that every mentor has to be someone senior to you. Over the years, some of my team members have also been my most valued mentors. Whenever I've moved

Meet a VIP

Identify a key person in your company whom you want to meet, and ask your boss to contact him or her on your behalf. Explain that all you want is a twenty-minute "get to know you" session. Almost anyone will meet you for twenty minutes! Your assignment, however, is to make certain that it is a productive twenty minutes, both for you and for the person who meets with you. Prepare diligently and send your résumé or bio in advance so that the person will have some background up front and you can focus the encounter by asking for advice on specific issues or areas. Assure the executive with whom you meet that you value his or her counsel. Later, try to arrange a follow-up meeting, in which you present the outcomes of the first meeting. If possible, report on the positive results of the executive's advice to you. If you persuade the other person that he or she was wise to have invested twenty minutes in you, you will have gone a long way toward recruiting a mentor.

into new areas in which I lacked core experience and expertise, I've sought and received "reverse coaching" from team members who were sometimes two or three levels lower in our organization. When I was a CIO, I benefited from regular coaching sessions with team members responsible for evaluating new technologies. They kept me ahead of the industry curve. I also arranged coaching sessions with our vendor management team, which kept me up to date on how our supplier partnerships were doing. When I visited with employees in the field, it was not just to hear them report to me. I wanted to learn from *them* how *they* supported our customers and what I could do to help them be more productive.

YOU ALSO NEED SPONSORS

Whereas a mentor advises and counsels you—very important—a sponsor actually reaches out to the world and actively advocates for you. In a corporate setting, an effective sponsor is someone who has a *seat at the table* where top-level hiring and promotion decisions are made. What you want is a senior, top-level executive who is willing to stand behind you and position you for new opportunities.

Women seem to have more difficulty, or perhaps more reticence, than men when it comes to finding sponsors. In fact, lack of sponsorship was one of the chief structural obstacles identified by the McKinsey researchers.[3] I saw this myself among the many hundreds of people I managed. Male employees often came to my office and asked me outright for recommendations and support. They also showed up to share the good news any time they'd won an award. My female staff hardly ever reported to me when they'd been recognized, even when it came time for them to turn in self-evaluations for performance reviews. Half the time I'd hear about it from other managers. I'm convinced that to them it felt like bragging.

If you've had trouble finding sponsors, it may just be that you haven't been proactive enough in enlisting them. Just about all the women leaders I interviewed for this book volunteered examples of sponsors who had advocated on their behalf, whether they used that word to describe them or not. Federal Reserve System CIO Lyn McDermid's first boss made sure she became the first woman in the Newport News Shipbuilding and Dry Dock Company Apprentice Program, kicking off her entire career. Jeanette Horan, CIO of IBM, made the leap to senior management because her boss took a chance on her—not so much because he knew her work firsthand (he was new in the role) but because she had several sponsors advocating to him on her behalf.

Having been in numerous senior executive roles, I fully appreciate that you must have someone to advocate for you and serve as your sponsor when the top-level jobs open up. Typically, there are many qualified candidates for each top job, and the competition can be brutal. Most important to keep in mind is that these jobs are very rarely chosen by one hiring manager. Usually, there is a selection committee comprising several senior executives. Although the process is tough, in the end, the chosen candidate is better off because he or she steps into the job with the support of at least a majority of those who served on the selection committee. You almost never even get in front of the selection committee unless you have a sponsor—a person who makes sure your name appears on the candidate list, who represents you, and who speaks up on your behalf.

When I was first chosen as an officer of my company, I was presented for the role along with many other qualified candidates. I was fortunate to have strong support from several of the people on the selection committee—which, by the way, was all male. There were, however, a few committee members who spoke out not so much against me, but in advocacy of their own candidate. It is naive to deny that politics does not enter into the committee's final choice. I was also told that, when I was up for discussion, several committee members voiced their belief that I did not have enough experience managing a large group.

There was some truth to this—but whether the objection arose more from factual truth or political circumstances, I never knew. In the end, however, a majority were convinced that I had excelled at everything I'd been given a chance to do, and that I should therefore be given this new opportunity. I am sure this outcome was due in no small measure to the sponsorship of one of the committee members, for whom I had worked directly. Without his strong vocal support, the position would never have been offered to me.

By the way, an effective sponsor doesn't just advocate for you when it's time for a promotion. You may need his or her support at a time when a particular opportunity does not work out—when, despite your best efforts, you find yourself at the center of a failing initiative. Failure does not have to be an end, and good sponsorship is a way to ensure that it won't be.

Although sponsors can usher you to the next level, it is significantly more difficult to recruit a sponsor and to develop a relationship with him or her than it is to recruit and cultivate a mentor. In the best-case scenario, a mentor develops into a sponsor over time. In my own personal experience, sponsors found me. If you want to be found, you need to dare to stand out, focus on delivering results in your present position, and make sure others are aware of your accomplishments.

Many times, the person most likely to serve as your sponsor is your boss. It is for this reason that many high-achieving women have told me that choosing your next boss is as important as choosing your next job. It is truly a strategic choice—a choice you make for the long term, a *career* move, not just a job decision.

Many executive women I have spoken with over the years have told me they would go so far as to recommend taking a less-than-ideal job if it clearly provided the opportunity to work with someone you could learn from, a person who seemed to have the makings of a great coach, mentor, and sponsor. It is always strategically valuable to have someone in your corner who sits at the table where decisions are made *and* who will speak up on your behalf. In fact, finding such a sponsor is critical to getting chosen for just about any senior executive position.

FIND ALLIES

There will be times when you really could use some help, but your mentor or sponsor isn't around. That is why your network should also include a circle of allies. Allies can be of long standing, or they can be recruited pretty much on the spot. They are colleagues—sometimes peers, sometimes a level or two below you, sometimes above—with whom you make common cause, either in general or on specific topics or issues.

There will be moments when you find that your voice is simply not heard. In my day, this happened a lot. I can remember many times when, in a large meeting in which I was the only woman, I would try to make a point, and then try several times again, without a single person acknowledging my comment. Then—within minutes, perhaps—a man would essentially repeat what I had said, and *his* words would launch a whole discussion. Somebody might even chime in with, "Oh, what a great idea!" Other times it was more subtle than that. A meeting would begin to wrap up with the leader's summary of the "good ideas" and "action items" the gathering had produced. One of my points would be mentioned on that summary list—only to be credited to one of the men in the room.

I don't believe these outcomes were the result of planned discrimination or a purposeful assault against me, the woman. Often they happened unconsciously. The makeup of the workplace was changing faster than the underlying cultural mindsets of the mixed group now sitting around that table.

Depending on your industry and where you live, many of you may still experience moments like this today. Even if you're fortunate enough to be in a more evolved professional culture, there will still be instances in which people don't hear your voice in a key moment. It doesn't need to be related to your gender. Maybe you won't have figured out the most compelling way to articulate your message. Maybe your message will simply be an unpopular one, however necessary or true it might be. Or maybe, for whatever reason, you'll simply lack confidence in that moment and others will sense it and respond accordingly.

These moments will come, and the good news is that there *is* a workaround. It is to recruit an ally. Plant this person in the meeting or activity during which you plan to introduce an idea or take an important stand. The ally's role is to second you. It is to comment positively on your statement. It is to ensure that your voice is heard—that it gets attention, and that you are credited with your idea.

Your ally does not necessarily have to be another woman; however, a woman is often the most obvious and natural choice. During my own tenure as a new VP, our company had one other woman at this level. We agreed that, whenever possible, each of us could count on there being "at least one other woman in the room." We also agreed that when one of us made a statement that others should hear, the other would break into the conversation to say she thought the other had made a good point. In these ways, we ensured that people with clout not only heard what we had to say but also credited it to us.

This pact and our process really did work. I often share this story with other women who complain about not being heard. Time and again, they come back and tell me how they adopted this strategy and that it worked for them too. What if you are the *only* woman at your level? Look for a progressive-minded man whom you feel comfortable asking to make this pact. You'll find one.

Taking the idea of allies more broadly, consider creating a peer support group. Author and CEO Keith Ferrazzi is a leading advocate of peer support and mentorship. In fact, he graciously mentored me on the writing of this book. In *Who's Got Your Back*, Keith coaches readers to create peer mentoring groups, which he calls Lifeline Groups.[4] Lifeline Groups emphasize shared leadership rather than the teacher-student dynamic of mentoring; members take turns holding the group accountable to its goals, meeting times, and rules of conduct.

Personally, I call my group my "posse." We have supported each other for years. It is made up of people who are at the same level as I am, but we share different perspectives and have varied skills and knowledge. It's very important to look for people who are different from you. I had one of the women I interviewed for this book tell me that she keeps her worst critic close by. This helps her be aware of all the possibilities and implications before deciding on a course of action. It is also good to look for people who will challenge, push, and *dare* you to do more than you ever thought possible.

THE FIRST LAW OF MOTION

Yes, it's hard to put yourself out there and make the first move to establish new relationships. Isaac Newton's First Law of Motion states that objects at rest remain at rest unless pushed. Inertia is a fact of life, but once you do push, you will find that 98 percent of those you approach will welcome the gentle nudge and will embrace the opportunity to speak with you and to get to know you. The next time you feel unsure about meeting someone new, remember that business—your business—is all about relationships, and relationships begin, grow, and are sustained by communication. Seize the opportunity. Start talking. Start listening. Respond. Turn every encounter into a productive relationship.

Dare to . . . Reach Out

Time to build your network! Which relationships do you need to build or strengthen? Use these action items to get started:

- Identify five people outside of your company who serve in a role that is similar to your own; research them online and reach out to initiate a relationship.
- Create a monthly networking opportunity. You could attend an event or conference, host a dinner, or organize a "brown bag" luncheon discussion at your company.
- Schedule a series of one-on-one meals with coworkers—this is a great way to recruit allies.
- Consider your boss: Is he or she a potential mentor or sponsor? Schedule a meeting to discuss your long-term goals; if he or she is responsive, use this interaction to launch a more formal mentoring relationship.

- Identify five other potential mentors and make a first step toward building a relationship with each one. Requesting a ten-minute meeting to get their advice on a specific issue is a great way to launch a conversation. Very few people will say no to ten minutes.
- Start a peer support group. You can find a free Lifeline Group starter kit on Keith Ferrazzi's Web site, at http://keithferrazzi.com/free-resource/whos-got-your-back. Sheryl Sandberg's Web site also offers free resources for launching peer support groups, which she calls Lean In Circles. Download them at http://leanin.org/circle-materials/.

CHAPTER EIGHT

DARE TO BE MORE THAN THE BOSS

Nurture Productive Relationships on the Front Line and Across the Organization

People are people first. They don't care what you know until they know you care.
MARTHA MCGILL, COO, MIAMI CHILDREN'S HOSPITAL

I once attended a senior executive event at which we were asked, "If you had a young person you cared a great deal about coming to work for our company, what single piece of advice would you give him or her?" Then we were broken into teams, asked to discuss the question, and told to report back to the group on our findings. A dozen teams of ten independently brainstormed the question. We were all surprised when every single team came back with precisely the same piece of advice: build a strong network of relationships with others *all across the company.*

Those relationships, internal but outside your own team, might not seem that important when you're at the junior level, but they become absolutely essential to earning executive leadership and then excelling once you're tapped. There will be times when you have to engage not just your team, but an entire division or divisions, across multiple constituencies, if you want to get the job done. A leader needs to be able to manage relationships as both a conductor and a first violinist—with broad strategy and one-on-one finesse.

Chapter Seven focused on cultivating allies, sponsors, and mentors to support you in your career, wherever it takes you. Here we'll explore more specifically the relationship skills and strategies needed to be an outstanding boss and agent of change, someone who is tasked with both leading teams and pushing initiatives at the organizational level.

The higher up the ladder you go, the less the job is about you, and the more it is about the quality of the team you build

---

The Mentors Speak: On Rallying Your Team

I'm a passionate person, and sometimes my passion gets in the way of effectiveness. So I've learned to check it a bit and channel my passion in ways that rally the troops. I've also learned that it isn't about me; it is about everyone else. Putting people first is absolutely the right thing to do.

Carol B. Tomé, CFO and executive VP of corporate services, The Home Depot

I've learned you can never tell someone too many times that they've done a good job. Recognition is free and it buys so much. When I want a certain kind of behavior repeated, I take the time to recognize it and celebrate it.

Robin Bienfait, former CIO, Research In Motion

I have struggled to be kinder, more compassionate, and more understanding with people. Whether it's in the workplace or at home, the struggle has always been between being right and being kind. In the long run, being kind is more important than being successful, but by the time one understands this simple truth, a great deal of damage may have been done. I daily remind myself to be more tolerant.

Loveleen Kacker, CEO, Tech Mahindra Foundation

around you. Not growing other leaders is among the worst kinds of performance failures you can make in the C-suite. Your greatest challenge as an executive is to not just be daring yourself but also find ways to inspire your employees and colleagues to dare—to lead them in a way that motivates them to bring their best, not because they have to, but because they care deeply.

THE VALUE OF "FRIENDRAISING"

Hala Moddelmog, president of Arby's, told me one of the most impressive stories I've ever heard of an executive deploying an organized, thoughtful relationship-building strategy to lead change. Hala was brought into her role in 2010 for a very specific reason: in the two years since the economic downturn in 2008, Arby's sales, profits, and morale had all been on the decline.

Hala knew the brand well; Arby's had been her first job out of graduate school. She believed 100 percent that the restaurant chain could be great and grow again, but she also saw her challenge: to regain the confidence of the one hundred thousand franchisees and employees, and, of course, the confidence of customers. "I was confident that with strong vision, good communication, and collaboration, we would be able to grow the brand," she says.

As a first step, Hala leveraged the expertise of Arby's franchisees and employees by setting up informal "get to know you" sessions. She traveled personally to visit the company's large franchisees and owners of single restaurants, asking them where they felt the company should focus its energy and strategies.

She then followed up on those in-person sessions with virtual communication, a weekly series of webinars, conferences, and e-mails to communicate the growth plan. "I wanted to make sure the franchisees understood what we were doing to grow their business and gain their buy-in and trust," she says. "Most important, I wanted to instill confidence about our plans to grow Arby's."

Finally, she put her "always-go-to" strategy into effect: hiring an excellent leadership team of passionate and smart people who work collaboratively and celebrate every win together. "This is a team that works very hard, but we also like to laugh and enjoy one another's company," Hala says.

The strategy worked. Hala led Arby's to seven consecutive quarters of sales growth in existing stores after four years of decline, introduced a new product line, and launched a new brand-positioning and ad campaign.

Kathleen Matthews, a news anchor who moved into the executive world of corporate PR at Marriot, calls this kind of outreach campaign to key constituents "friendraising." She learned the hard way how important it is to build relationships—that is, to friendraise—before pushing initiatives that require many people to change the way they work and think. Building those relationships is key to understanding the context, or the culture, within which you're operating.

Kathleen started her new role with what was regarded by colleagues as a major coup: she convinced CEO Bill Marriot that he should have a blog to talk directly to customers in a friendly, informal way. Bill Marriot, "seventy-five years old but intrepid," according to Kathleen, loved the idea of jumping into the world of social media. Together they launched the blog in a matter of weeks.

Emboldened by her success in bringing an idea so quickly to fruition, Kathleen moved forward on a number of other new initiatives. But unbeknownst to her, she was starting to step on toes. "My agenda for change was not necessarily widely shared, and I didn't know the organization well enough to understand all the fiefdoms I should be visiting," she says. Rather than enlisting allies, she alienated some senior executives, who, convinced she wouldn't last in the position, were determined to wait out her time at the company.

"Finally, I hit the wall and failed—for the first time in my career. I could not get an initiative through the organization," recalls Kathleen. "But I quickly realized my mistake, and I started working on the relationship building that I had been too busy to pursue when I first arrived at the company. Today, I better understand the importance of friendraising when you want to get big things done in a corporation."

SPEND TIME ON THE FRONT LINE

There is a big difference between people who are good at their specific jobs and people who can lead others. Skill in building relationships and managing people develops through experience and depends on your willingness to listen to, learn from, and relate to others. This is the reason why many highly competent people, who are good at their jobs, never progress into C-level roles.

In *Coffee at Luna's*, business strategist Chuck Martin offers the message that, as a leader, your job is to understand what issues and challenges each of your team members must contend with.[1] Your job is not to do the team's work yourself. Once you acquire the necessary understanding, your next task is to remove obstacles that get in the way of the team's work. Both of these jobs require that you *listen* to the members of the team, including their good ideas about how to improve the work processes. In large organizations, it is often difficult to get this kind of feedback from everyone, but just by taking the time to walk around or to convene focus groups, you flush out many of the most useful ideas.

Spending time with frontline employees and with customers is so important that I used to list it as a job requirement in the "performance expectations" I would distribute to all of my direct reports. Some protested: "I don't have time to do this." My response was firm: "You need to make this your top priority," I would say. "It's a big deal for employees to have someone from the executive office spend time with them. They're inspired, and you will learn how the tools your team provides affect our customers and our business. You will also learn what we need to be doing in the executive suite to better support them, which is, after all, our primary job."

The information that comes from direct contact with front-line employees is vital and cannot be gathered by staying in the corporate office. You yourself have to invest time on the front line. Sam Walton, founder of Walmart, was famous for regularly visiting his stores, and he required every senior leader to do the same. His belief was that those out front, dealing with customers on a daily basis, were naturally and obviously in the best position to give advice on what could be done to improve service and better meet the needs of customers.

I know from personal experience how much I learned by being on the front line with employees. There is no substitute for seeing and experiencing your company's business for yourself. There is also no better way to improve morale and build trust. Any time I met with employees, I asked:

"What do we need to be doing to help you?"
"Do you feel that we are providing you with the tools and information you need to be effective in your job?"
"Do you have any ideas about how we can improve as a team?"

Occasionally, I would not get any feedback. When I didn't, I took it as an indication that we needed to create a climate in our organization that was more conducive to candor. Most of the time, however, the information was invaluable and eminently actionable. There were times when the ideas could not be implemented—often for regulatory or compliance

Move Beyond Compliance to Cooperation

Company policy, directives, and initiatives succeed or fail depending on whether or not employees embrace them. Creating understanding is the key to encouraging employees to embrace policies voluntarily and consistently, rather than just when they fear reprisal. Make it a leadership priority to keep communication lines wide open and active. Be transparent with those around you. Open your door and climb down from anything resembling an ivory tower. The more people know about your goals and how you plan to get them accomplished, the more enthusiastically they will support you.

reasons—but even in these instances, I had an opportunity to explain why that was the case. With better understanding, employees embraced policies instead of fighting against them.

Getting in touch with the front line will only become more important as formerly hierarchical corporations become increasingly flat. In the future, organizations will need more leaders who know how to inspire a team and help them come to a group conclusion. They will also need more leaders who know how to grow other leaders.

ALWAYS LET YOUR CALMER HEAD PREVAIL

Looking back on my own experience, I can recall too many occasions on which I've let my emotions get the best of me, not only in business but in my personal life, too. In the course of my interviews, I learned I certainly wasn't alone in having those regrets.

Kat Cole, president of Cinnabon, told me about a time when she was running a large project and an executive, looking for shortcuts, trumped some of her decisions. "I was devastated, because I knew the frustration that would cause our employees, but I handled it poorly," she says. "What I thought of as passion came across as immaturity and emotion. I learned that it's not just what you say, but how you say it in the moment that can affect not only the work, but others' perceptions of your ability to 'hang with the big boys.'"

Passion is a very good thing when it's pointed in the right direction, but undirected passion, the energy of rage or panic, can wreak havoc. It may prompt you to say things you will regret, and once a thing is said, there's no taking it back. As a leader, you need exceptional emotional management. Others are watching you. Lose your cool, and you turn up the emotional volume for your whole team.

Stay Calm and Give Do-Overs

Words are not retractable, and it's your responsibility to think about the impact of what you will say before you say it. Think your words through, as if they are going to appear on the home page of *Bloomberg*. The same goes for e-mails. When confronted with highly emotional situations at work, take four steps:

1. Take a deep breath—and keep breathing. You're going to get through this.
2. Get everyone focused on the facts—determining them, reporting them, and discussing them. Facts take the emotion out of most any situation. You may learn that you have correct information, or you may discover new information that helps you and your team better handle the situation. Things—situations, errors—can be fixed. Personalities cannot. Focus on the things, the facts.
3. Assuming the situation allows the time, talk it out with a mentor, sponsor or someone else you trust.
4. Resist the impulse for immediate action. Unless you find yourself in a truly pressing emergency, take some time. Allow emotions—yours included—to settle down before responding or taking action.

At the same time, give others the benefit of the doubt. Always accept a compliment graciously, even if it comes out awkwardly or in the form of backhanded praise. Pretend they expressed themselves in the best way possible. Become the kind of person people love to support and compliment.

The bottom line is, it's up to you, as a leader, to be the bigger person. Treating people right will pay dividends; being callous or hotheaded can ruin you. Rebecca Jacoby told me about a time when her communication style almost took her career off course. She had recently been promoted to leading her team, with whose members she had good relationships. Then the group merged with another, whose people had never worked with her before. Within a month, the new team members had filed formal complaints against her.

"I was devastated and hurt, although for whatever reason I intuitively understood that I did not want to be defensive. I listened to everything they had to say. I realized I needed to use a softer approach and understand how I come across," she says. "I would say I was almost too professional—not allowing my personality to surface and giving direct feedback without recognizing my manner of communication. This was a turning point for me as a leader and a lesson that has stuck with me my whole career."

Develop a habit of communicating at a level that is intimate as well as inspiring and uplifting. This is not as difficult as it sounds. Uplift and inspire those around you by communicating to *them* your certainty of *their* importance to *you* and to the enterprise. You don't need to make flowery speeches, and you certainly don't need to counterfeit gratitude. There is no reason to. The truth is that your peers and your reports really *are* crucially important to you and the enterprise. Communicate this fact enthusiastically and frequently—you really can't do it too much.

Become the Boss You'd Like to Have

As a boss, much of your focus is devoted to observing and improving your employees' performance: Are they doing what they're supposed to do, when they're supposed to, and with excellence? When it comes to evaluating your own performance, your vision may be a bit more fuzzy. I've found that the following exercise creates an immediate and dramatic perspective shift, revealing exactly where your leadership is falling short and how to remedy that.

1. Write a description of what your perfect boss would be like—how would he or she greet you in the morning, make requests, handle mistakes, and so on? Let the list be long.

2. Look over your list with this question in mind: How many of these things are you doing for your employees? If you are like me, you will find this step to be a wake-up call to do more for your team members.

3. For items on which you know you're remiss, brainstorm ways to build those qualities or actions into your leadership style. Put the ideas in writing, and keep them handy on your computer desktop or on a sticky note for a few weeks until you develop new habits.

You will be amazed by the positive impact that you as a leader can have on other people, and by the transformational impact they, in turn, will have on you and your endeavors. Happy people who feel their efforts are recognized are more productive. Heed the wisdom of cosmetics industry executive Mary Kay Ash, who said, "Everyone has an invisible sign hanging from their neck saying, 'Make me feel important.' Never forget this message when working with people."

The fact that your employees look up to you and respect you as an authority figure means that everything you say, both your accolades and your critiques, is amplified. That's a big responsibility—and also an opportunity. Make the most of it.

WHEN TO HAVE TOUGH CONVERSATIONS

Being the boss means having some tough conversations. For starters, at some point, every boss will have to end her official relationship with an employee who's not living up to the responsibilities of his or her role. No one enjoys having to fire anyone, but it's an important part of keeping your team's relationships healthy and productive. You also owe it to the failing employee. You're not being a friend or a good boss by letting employees continue in a role in which they're unable or unwilling to succeed. Sometimes firing them or letting them go is the fastest way to help *them* fail forward.

But I know it's not easy, especially at first. As an SVP, I myself saw so many people (women and men, but more often the women) go through circus-like contortions to keep questionable employees on staff. They often said they hoped to "coach" the failing employee, but at what cost? From a distance it was plain these were people who needed to go. Dozens of the women I interviewed for this book told me that they had experienced a time, sometimes more than one, when putting off firing an employee had negative implications, for their company and their career.

Telecom executive Diana Einterz's self-described worst mistake wasn't a "drastic catastrophe," she says, "but it came close." Earlier in her career, Diana, who is now the head of Americas for Orange Business Services, a $500 million enterprise, made a bad hire for a significant role, and then waited too long to replace him. The signs that he had to go were all there, but she came up with reasons to delay rather than taking decisive action: she wasn't close enough to the business, didn't want to inflict yet another management change, wanted to give him the benefit of the doubt, and so on. "They were laudable motives, but, in the end, I allowed others to suffer," she says.

"The damage he did took me years to repair. People resigned. The business declined. Morale suffered."

The more confidence you have in your judgment and intuition, the harder it is to rationalize delaying the inevitable to avoid conflict. Says Diana, "I have learned to listen to that voice inside my head that tells me things that, maybe, I don't always want to hear or to face. I have learned that, even when the decision is difficult or painful, it is my responsibility to take the action and be swift."

Dell CIO Adriana Karaboutis is another who told me she had once fallen into the trap of trying to "change" bad employees and hurting her team as a result. Adriana ultimately figured out who should stay or go in this way: "I started assessing whether employees were transformers, contributors, watchers, or detractors relative to the goals and objectives of the organization. Transformers and contributors are helpful to the organization, and watchers can be coached to be helpful. Detractors, however, need to be moved to other organizations or even exited," says Adriana. When dealing with a detractor, take corrective action as quickly as possible.

Finally, work to overcome the instinct to avoid conflict by postponing difficult conversations. When you're having trouble with a direct report, a colleague, even a boss, don't wait—talk to him or her about it right away. Otherwise you may feel your frustration build to the point where you either explode inappropriately or vent with another colleague—either of which can be damaging to the original relationship.

Kim Greene, president and CEO of Southern Company Services, is no shrinking violet when it comes to making and communicating tough decisions. She's had to restructure many groups—bringing in the right talent, letting go of the wrong talent, and doing it all within tight timelines and with attention to the strict regulatory and legal issues of her industry. "I have had to make many decisions that are not popular," she says, "but are the right thing to do for the long-term success of the company."

As unflappable as she is today, Kim told me about one memorable communication misstep from early in her career, one that has stuck with her ever since. While working on a project, she was frustrated with the performance of her colleague, whom we'll call "Sam." Rather than sit down and solve the problem with him, she vented about it in an e-mail to a third colleague. Just as she hit "send"—I think you know what's coming—she realized that she had addressed the e-mail to Sam himself. At that point she knew she needed to take action quickly. She immediately sought him out in person and engaged him in a conversation.

Kim managed to work things out amicably with Sam, and they left with a better relationship and (to Sam at least!) a funny story. What turned out to be a minor slipup nevertheless taught Kim two important lessons that she gladly shared: "First, I committed to always address issues professionally with my colleagues. Second, I always reread e-mails and carefully check whom they are being sent to before I hit 'send.' If there is something in the e-mail that I wouldn't want the public to read on the front page of the newspaper, then I don't send it."

E-mail, for all its value, creates some of business's worst communication failures. Before you hit "send" on any message of import, ask yourself whether it's a conversation better had in person or on the phone.

IT TAKES EARS TO BUILD RELATIONSHIPS

Friendraising, both inside and outside of your firm, will teach you the art of listening. I'm a talker, so it was hard for me to heed my father's advice when I was heading off to my first job. But it was golden nonetheless. "Do more listening than speaking," he told me, "and you'll go far in this world." Years earlier, a teacher had put it to me another way: "You have two ears and one mouth, so listen twice as much as you talk."

Listening is a critical skill for any leader, and—fortunately for me—a learnable one. I was never a naturally patient listener, but thanks to my father and others, I knew enough to take steps to change that. Learning to listen, and to listen actively, made me a more effective leader in many areas of my life. Be honest with yourself. If you conclude that you're not a very good listener, take steps to become one.

To demonstrate good listening, you should always follow the other person's message with a thoughtful response. People will trust you and share more and more openly with you if they know you will listen to them. How do they know you are listening? By the responses you make and the questions you ask.

Every year our company administered a survey about our corporate culture. As the CIO, I received all of the anonymous input from my team. I read every single response and tried to discern the top themes evident in the information. When I discussed these themes with my managers, I would point out, "Some of these things we can't do anything about. They're out of our control." However, identifying the issues we could effectively address, we set out to seize opportunities and to fix resolvable problems. It was abundantly clear to the entire team that we leaders had listened and that we cared. Even more important, our employees understood that *they* mattered and that *their* input was important to our enterprise.

On one occasion, our leadership team tried to make changes to reduce costs and generally speed up our processes. In concept, this was certainly the right idea. But in execution, the changes we made saved no money and, in fact, slowed us down by expanding bureaucracy instead of eliminating it (as we had intended to do). The redesigned processes worked quite well for big projects, but they introduced too many layers of bureaucracy for the smaller jobs. The fact was that most of our projects were in the small category. Thanks to the feedback we received, however, we knew what had to be done. We used the new processes only on the few large projects, while streamlining steps for our many smaller projects. Listening to feedback from those closest to the work helped us improve the overall work flow dramatically. And it built trust, relationships, and team-work across the organization.

The more experience you gain as a manager, the more you will encounter a truly remarkable thing: employee satisfaction and dissatisfaction are not typically about money. People want to work for someone who listens to them and who cares about them. It is therefore important for business leaders to be compassionate and to demonstrate that they care about the people on their team. In *The Speed of Trust,* Stephen Covey writes that only 42 percent of workers believe that management cares about them at all, and 29 percent believe management cares about developing not them, but their *skills.*[2] Terrible statistics! But there is a big opportunity to change this in your own organization by doing a better job of listening and responding to your employees.

Listen—then take the next natural step beyond listening, which is *recognition.* I used to spend time in our operations center, far from the executive suites. I well knew that the people who worked there and at the technology help desks were our most underappreciated employees. They were, in fact, almost invisible—unless, of course, you had a problem. *Then* they seemed like the most important people in the whole organization.

To ensure 24/7 support of our work, employees in the operations center work in shifts. This means that many of them miss corporate events, especially at holiday times. I often called the center or dropped by on holidays to thank our employees who were working instead of spending time with friends or family.

Little things mean a lot. Most people in leadership are so busy getting the work done that they forget about taking care of their team, which includes showing gratitude for the individual contributions that come in a variety of forms: volunteering for projects, taking risks with new ideas, working odd hours, taking on a controversial or pioneering role, or trying a new process.

SPEAK THE LANGUAGE OF ENCOURAGEMENT

In the lingering aftermath of the Great Recession, many employees are struggling. Burdened by stress from shouldering multiple jobs—often with much overtime but little or no additional compensation—they may feel demotivated. As their supervisor, you can and must turn morale around. You can lead your team from demoralization to hope. You can dispel resentment by persuading employees that they are part of one of the best places to work. Begin by encouraging everyone on your team and acknowledging their achievements. Look for the positive possibilities, the means of promoting the collective good, and reach for them.

Never underestimate the power of encouragement. Recognition costs nothing. It doesn't take a lot of time, but it does speak volumes. The value of recognition to an employee really hit home for me one day when I was on a field visit in Rome, Georgia. As I was walking the halls, a man tapped me on the shoulder. I was his boss's boss's boss, if you can imagine. "I've been at this company thirty years, and I want to show you the thing I'm most proud of," he told me. We went to his office, and he showed me a trophy he had received from management for contributing an idea to the company that had made it all the way through to patent. He was clearly proud of his contribution, but beyond that, the company's recognition of it mattered. The trophy had become the proudest milestone of this man's career. This inexpensive token of appreciation demonstrated that small gestures yield significant results.

Taking the time to recognize someone else's helpful actions makes a huge, positive impact. Recognition is what we all need, and a good leader can provide it in such little things as a "thank you," a "well done," or a bright smile. These gestures don't have to come from the boss. Some of the most inspirational notes I received as a leader were from employees on my team. Everyone appreciates a little pat on the back, and this can go a long way in helping to build a trusting and supportive relationship.

Dare to . . . Improve Your Internal Relationships

Take these steps to make your relationships across the organization stronger and more productive:

- *Get away from your desk.* Schedule meetings in the offices of people who report to you. You learn a great deal about people by meeting in their office—from the photos on their desk to the overall work environment they've created. Or get out of the office entirely. Touring facilities or walking around your campus with an employee radiates approachability and can be a great learning opportunity.

- *Practice appreciation.* Each week, write an e-mail to an employee or colleague with the express purpose of acknowledging his or her good work or anything he or she has done that's been truly helpful.

- *Cross silos.* Schedule a meeting once a month with someone from outside of your functional area or division. Swap information and compare your perspectives on what in your organization needs changing.

- *Temporarily become a customer service representative.* Spend a few hours getting as close to the customer or client as you can—even if that means working on the floor or manning a customer service line. The experience not only will give you new insight into whom you're serving but also will put you in the shoes of the folks on the front line.

CHAPTER NINE

DARE TO BE THERE—FOR OTHERS

Give Back and Invite Others to Join You at the Top

Help others achieve their dreams and you will achieve yours.
LES BROWN, AMERICAN BUSINESSMAN

So far, we've focused on getting you to dare to develop the skills you need, to take the risks that lead to great reward. Once you are a leader, however, the single greatest thing you will do is grow other leaders. So many times in the business world, amid the meetings and projects and financial reports, you wonder, "Am I really making a difference?"

Looking back on my career, there's one place I do *know* that I mattered: I made a difference for the people who worked on my teams and whom I mentored, both the men and the women. There's nothing that makes me happier than having former employees come to me and tell me that something I did, said, or taught them made their career bloom.

To go back to where we started for a moment: women today make up roughly half the general workforce, yet they hold less than 15 percent of the executive roles in the Fortune 500. Instead of being glum about the gap, I like to think of the statistics as evidence of just how much more room there is for women at the top. *A whole lot.* And the more women who are at the top, the better—for you, and for all the women who would like to ascend with and after you.

Corporate culture still needs to change, and the only way to do it is by changing the culture from the inside. In a recent LinkedIn poll, the number one obstacle cited as limiting women's progression in business was institutional barriers.[1] If these barriers are going to be removed, we must be more active in identifying them, and making them go away. It will take leadership on an individual basis to make this happen. You've got to be the chicken and the egg, getting rid of all those old rules, obsolete perceptions, and worn-out habits that threaten to crowd out the extraordinary in life. Thinking back to thirty years ago, when I and others started making our way to the executive suite in our bow-tied "ladies' office wear," the glass ceiling was thick and opaque—I wasn't even sure what the other side would look like. Although the journey was tough, I can't tell you what satisfaction it gives me today to see young women enjoying a broad range of opportunities and freedom in how they model leadership.

But even today, for every woman who shares your desire to make change at the top, there may be another who is holding back. She might join you, if only she had a terrific role model to guide her—someone who could show her by example how to be an executive and a mother, and be nourished by both roles; how to develop a leadership style that isn't masculine or feminine but distinctly her own; how to command respect without surrendering the instinct to care; and how to volunteer herself for stretch challenges and knock them out of the park with courage and the willing help of trusted, gifted colleagues.

The women who contributed to this book are exactly these kinds of role models. And you can be one too, right now. You have everything inside you to become an outstanding leader in your chosen career and a role model in your community. I hope the lessons in this book have helped you recognize that.

So as my final appeal, I dare you to be there for others.

BE A MENTOR, STARTING *NOW*

We need more women at the top. Gender-biased mind-sets and perceptions are not overcome by ethical pleas and business arguments alone. They are overcome by the increased presence of women in leadership positions. This means that we need more women who, from positions of real decision-making power, will speak up and advocate for other women, and who will step up to provide the coaching, the mentoring, and the sponsorship for the rising generation of corporate women—and the men, too! We are thankfully well beyond "us versus them." We need to serve as models for *all* leaders, male and female, but your guidance and sponsorship will be particularly important for the women in the organization who are struggling to figure out where they fit.

Judging by the numbers, we women are already doing a better job than men when it comes to a willingness to develop the talent of others. Sixty-five percent of women who received career development support are now developing new talent, compared to 56 percent of men who received support; and 73 percent of the women developing new talent are developing women, compared to only 30 percent of men, reported Catalyst.[2] So much for what Catalyst calls "the oft-cited 'Queen Bee' myth," which says that women are not just reluctant to provide career support to other women, they even go out of their way to undermine them. The numbers say no.

The numbers also show that mentoring others pays off, and not just in the sense of increased life satisfaction. Catalyst found that high-potential leaders, male and female, who were developing a protégé had $25,075 in "additional compensation between 2008 and 2010."[3] Speculating about why in a press release, Catalyst noted that it "may be that developing other talent creates more visibility and a following within the organization for the high-potentials who are doing the developing, which leads to greater reward and recognition for the extra effort."[4] A 2006 Gartner Research study of one thousand Sun Microsystems employees found that mentees were promoted five times more frequently than employees not in formal mentoring—and *mentors* were promoted *six* times more frequently than their nonmentoring peers.[5]

Few people exhibit more the power of transformative mentoring than Helene Lollis, the president of Pathbuilders, which partners with *Fortune*-ranked organizations to develop high-performing people through mentoring, executive development programs, and consulting. Since 2002, she has shared leadership (and ownership) of the company with two female partners.

In the late 1990s Helene was a chemical engineer at Amoco and a mentee in one of Pathbuilders programs. "The gentleman who I was matched with is still my mentor. He had an incredible amount of influence on the path of my career. There is no question that with his guidance my career blossomed." Helene was so strongly affected by her mentoring experience that when she heard the owners of Pathbuilders were exiting the business, she knew she had to act.

"I felt that the Pathbuilders program couldn't go away. Despite never having worked in a small business environment, I joined up with my two partners, who are also alumnae of the program, and we bought the company. The timing for me was right, because Amoco had been acquired by BP, and I had decided to leave the company in order to stay in Atlanta." The "dare" that Helene and her two partners took paid off. The company is thriving, with clients from such major brands as Verizon Wireless, Kimberly-Clark, and Turner Broadcasting. In fact, I first met Helene because Southern Company, my former employer, is a client.

"We know we change people and companies every day. There have been times that I've watched a room of mentors meeting with their mentees and been overcome with emotion," says Helene. "I couldn't personally give these women what they need, but through Pathbuilders we can create the environment and match them all with exactly the mentor who can. It is unbelievably rewarding."

You will find that mentorship *is* unbelievably rewarding— and, on top of that, the benefits to your own leadership advancement will be tangible.

The Mentors Speak: On Mentoring

I have been serving as a mentor for up-and-coming women for over fifteen years, and each year it becomes more rewarding for me personally. We all can learn from each other. I have seen a big improvement in my listening skills and in my ability to connect with other people. I see some aspect of me in every mentee, and it helps me to see where I can continue to grow myself. That is the greatest gift we can give ourselves . . . to keep learning and growing.

Jill Ratliff, SVP of human resources,
Assurant Specialty Property

One of the purposes of being a mentor is to help the mentee look at situations through a different lens. A manager may just want her to achieve the goals of the job. I'm a safe harbor to explore what else she wants to do and what she needs to learn. Answering tough questions and sharing best practices also keeps me on my toes and my own skates sharp.

Michelle Boyea, VP of talent acquisition,
McKesson Corporation

We have a responsibility to give back. But what also drives me to mentor is that, coming up as a CEO, especially a female CEO for a tech company in the South, I made so many mistakes early on. I wish I had had someone I could have spoken to back then. Now I want to be that person for others.

Karen Robinson Cope, SVP of sales and
marketing, NanoLumens

MENTORING MAKES YOU A BETTER LEADER

They say that a good teacher learns from her students. Well, some of my best leadership learning experiences have come from relationships in which I was the mentor. Mentoring makes you conscious of your own expertise, which not only builds confidence but also allows you to refine your process. I was once meeting with a young high-potential employee who noted that I had worked in many very different areas of the company. She asked me if I had a standard way I operated when I was dropped into a totally new department. After a few moments of thought I realized that I did. I told her I always met with my new direct reports, asking for their perspective on what was going well and what needed to be fixed. I'd ask what was the best way for me to communicate with them and what I could do to help. Next I'd meet with the top customers and get their perspective. After rattling off a long list of my go-to onboarding activities, I realized that over the years I had developed a thirty-day launch plan for success, ready anytime I went into a new job. This was "expertise" I hadn't even realized I had, and now suddenly it was available to help this young woman.

Mentoring also can give a leader valuable new perspective, and make her sensitive to others' experience. Helene and her team recently had "a good laugh" thanks to a story passed on by one of her longtime clients, a woman who has mentored with Pathbuilders for years. "She had been listening to a group of mentees talking about something that all their bosses did, something that held them back but additionally was just really annoying," said Helene. "This woman listened sympatheti-cally—but left the session shaking her head. 'I realized that I was doing exactly the thing they were complaining about with all *my* direct reports! What an eye-opener,' she said."

A mentoring relationship with someone from a different background or generation can help you see your organization, even your industry, with fresh eyes. That's vital, because doing so grows increasingly difficult the longer you've been in the business. I was once mentoring a young woman from the operations division of my company. At the end of a session, I asked her to share some insights on my division, which at the time was IT. She told me quite candidly that my group had a reputation of telling people what they couldn't do versus what was possible. As a result, we were seen as being backward, instead of forward thinking and innovative.

I knew she was right. Our team was constantly meeting with technologists and had a good handle on what was coming three, four, or five years down the pike—but that wasn't something we were communicating. In our conversations with employees, we were often the "no" people. We had to be: we had compliance, security, and budget issues that required us to be fairly dictatorial about the way employees used technology.

So I asked for her advice on what she would do to change our image while being saddled with these issues. Her advice was excellent. She suggested that we consciously make an effort to show people what was coming in the way of new technology. Even if we couldn't unroll these technologies yet, we could give employees the comfort of knowing that we were looking forward and considering the impact they might have on our business. That's exactly what we started doing, and as a result, employees became much more willing to respect our mandates while volunteering ideas for the future.

Everyone has something to teach you, and it may not just be about business. I had one mentee who had her children early in life, whereas I had mine later. We found that I could coach her on work while she provided me with great advice on child care. She was, for example, an expert on how to find the perfect nanny, and she had many contacts to help me with this process.

MAKING THE MATCH

Serial entrepreneur Karen Robinson Cope told me she didn't start mentoring until she became a CEO in the early 1990s. "At that point I was much more in the public eye and there was more press, so I was approached more often. At the time I was one of very few women CEOs in the Southeast. And the ones like me who had raised venture money you could count on one hand."

Karen's experience is typical—we don't start mentoring until we have enough professional clout that young hopefuls seek us out. And that's not entirely a bad thing: as in any kind of adult education, the mentoring relationship is most effective when the student is self-motivated by the desire to learn. According to Helene from Pathbuilders, the most successful mentoring relationships are mentee driven. "For us what really drives a match is discovering a mentee's core developmental needs, those three or four things that if she can get right will move her to the next level."

That is to say, you can't always choose your protégés; the ideal circumstance is that they choose you. What you *can* do immediately is become the kind of boss, colleague, and friend who makes clear that she's open to supporting others. As we move up the ladder at work, with increasing pressures and demands on our time, the business of business sometimes makes it hard to be human. We're so focused on the project, the planning, the disaster around the bend, that our ability to be present for our people diminishes. Fight that. Take time with your employees to slow down. Ask questions. Create an environment in which they know your door or your desk is open to them, and for more than discussing their next deadline. Doing so will create opportunities for informal mentoring at every stage of your career, and give you your pick of protégés when that time comes.

Informal Versus Formal Mentoring

With informal mentoring:

- Connection drives interaction.
- Relationships evolve naturally.
- Individuals self-select.
- Meetings happen as opportunities arise.

With formal mentoring:

- Structure drives participation and purposeful discussion.
- Connections are created that may not occur naturally.
- Clear matching and topical discussions increase engagement.
- There is a defined start and stop.

Of course, that doesn't mean you should lavish time and attention on everyone. Be selective. Look for mentees who combine competence with passion—people who have a sense of mission; who want to make the company a better place; and who want, for that matter, to make the *world* a better place. Take a cue from Pathfinders and consider whether you're a good fit to help a mentee with her most pressing developmental needs.

To help you avoid typical pitfalls, I asked Helene if she could identify the top reasons she's seen mentor-mentee relationships fail. The first is present when there's a mismatch of expectations on anything from logistics to the level of formality in the relationship, so make sure you are clear up front about the structure and depth of support you can offer. The second pitfall is practical: sometimes relationships get tripped up due to conflicts in scheduling and simple logistics, and then never get back on track.

Finally, make sure to look to your mentee to define what she'd like to achieve through the relationship, on what timeline.

Helene says that a third common contributor to failed mentoring partnerships is mentees who fail to develop specific goals. Without specific objectives, it's impossible for either of you to evaluate whether your time together is creating any forward momentum, leaving little incentive to stick with the relationship.

MENTORING EFFECTIVELY

My most successful mentoring relationships have been those in which the mentees managed the relationship. They took the initiative to schedule the meetings. They came prepared with a focused list of issues to discuss with me, and they always began the meeting by telling me what they had done to follow up on any advice I had given in earlier sessions. I can tell you that nothing is more frustrating than having someone in whom you invest hours and energy tell you she "had not had time" to follow up on something you had advised her to do.

My mentees and I quickly learned that once the relationship is well developed, technology becomes a terrific and time-saving aid to efficient communication. I've had lots of successful career discussions with mentees via voice mail and e-mail. Time is of the essence, so finding ways to leverage asynchronous communication is essential to great mentoring relationships.

Make sure to look for opportunities to become a sponsor to the mentees you feel are deserving of your advocacy. One of my favorite mentees did an excellent job keeping me informed of moments when my sponsorship was needed. She would frequently leave me a voice mail with an update on what position she was being considered for, who the hiring manager was, and what she needed me to do to help. I would take this message and act on it by making calls or sending an e-mail with an endorsement. If I had any intelligence concerning the position

The Mentee's Role

The mentee should always take primary responsibility for setting up and driving the agenda in a mentoring session. Here's what a formal agenda might include:

- Review of action items from previous session(s)
- Recent mentee actions or accomplishments that the mentor should know about
- Ideas about how the mentor can help the mentee: recommendations for training or experiences; people she needs to meet and to whom the mentor is willing and able to make introductions
- Discussion of problem areas in which the mentor may have experience that can help guide the mentee
- Time spent setting up the next session date and drawing up a clear list of action items to be completed by the mentor and mentee before that next session

in question, I would call back and either talk to her or leave *her* a voice mail with the tips I had.

When you meet with your mentee, your first priority is to listen. When the mentee needs help with a decision or describes a struggle, don't be prescriptive. Instead, start by asking questions. Karen explains, "I know I learn best when I can process something myself. I also don't assume that I know more than the mentee. That's my leadership style overall. First I ask questions for clarity, then I ask questions that help lead the person down a particular path of thinking. I'll share my experience, but the model is, 'Have you thought about this . . . ?' not 'Here's the answer.'"

Although you may be the one with all the experience, it's really up to your mentee to provide her own answers. You're there to share, not to dictate, and to serve as her guide, not as her boss.

GIVE BACK EARLY

People often ask me to mentor them. The first question I ask in response is, "Whom are *you* mentoring?" Many times the reply is something to the effect of, "I'm not advanced enough or experienced enough in my career to mentor someone." To this, I respond that there are many opportunities to mentor and give back in addition to those at work. Volunteering to coach others in your community is a great way to enhance your leadership capabilities even when you're still green in the world of business.

The skills you develop working in the nonprofit world are easily portable to a corporate environment. In many cases, women tell me they have a difficult time getting their first supervisory role because they don't have any experience leading others. Don't miss an opportunity to demonstrate this type of leadership by volunteering in the community. It is a genuine opportunity to do well by doing good.

Volunteer Your Time

Opportunities to build coaching and mentoring skills are easy to find outside of your company, and even outside of the business community, no matter where you are in your career. Become a volunteer!

- Use the Internet to research local nonprofit organizations.
- Try a tool like VolunteerMatch (www.volunteermatch.org), which lists opportunities by city.
- Ask your network—what groups do people already work with, or have connections to? A warm introduction will help if you'd like to offer a nonprofit any skills—say, business coaching or individual mentoring—that might be outside its standard volunteer program.

MAKE AN UNBREAKABLE CHAIN

Share your knowledge freely, and make sure that one of the most important lessons you impart is that mentees, too, must in turn pay it forward. You are not just mentoring or sponsoring an employee to fill the next slot above her. You are helping create a workplace environment in which well-qualified women rise as naturally to the top as well-qualified men do—without gender even entering into the discussion.

Your actions will have an impact beyond your wildest possible imagination. When I interviewed Karen for this book, she had just experienced a poignant encounter with a mentee she met in 2000 after she was named Woman of the Year by the Technology Association of Georgia and the Women in Technology organization. She had mentored Jackie Brieter off and on for several years until the two lost track of each other. Just before our interview, Karen attended a meeting that brought together several local business leaders, most of them women, and was surprised to find Jackie among them.

"We had originally met at a little BBQ place where I've had more mentoring sessions than anywhere else in town. It's a hole-in-the-wall, centrally located with comfortable booths and no pretensions," says Karen. "She had some questions about whether she should stay or leave the large corporation where she was then employed. I asked her some questions to help her think it through."

When they met again, Jackie immediately reminded Karen of the advice she had given her twelve years prior back at the BBQ place, and confirmed that it had been instrumental in putting her on the path to where she was, as CIO of Emory University Business School, loving what she was doing. "But that wasn't the best part," says Karen. "What really moved me was that Jackie said that in the years since, she's made it a point to mentor young women. That's the impact that our meeting had. When you hear that, it's such a rewarding feeling. There's nothing else like it."

Make Time for Mentoring

Frequently women tell me, "I'd love to mentor someone, but I just don't have time." Informal mentorship doesn't have to be time consuming. You just need to be creative about how you fit it in. Some ideas that have worked for the women I mentor include the following:

- Meet in person quarterly and use the phone or video calling on Skype (www.skype.com) for more frequent meetings.
- Schedule a recurring "Friday fifteen" for weekly or biweekly check-ins—you'd be surprised how much value you can provide in fifteen minutes, if the mentee prepares questions in advance.
- Ask mentees to join you in activities that are already on your schedule, such as professional events, lectures, or workout sessions.
- Try group mentoring sessions: introduce several mentees to each other and encourage them to support each other as well.

When you choose to mentor someone, understand that you will change that person's life. But also know that you will do much more than that. In changing that life, you are changing her company, and in changing her company, you're evolving her industry as well as the society and culture in which her company and industry operate. Finally, you are changing the life of every woman to whom she pays it forward.

And in the process, you are changing yourself.

LOOK BEYOND *YOUR* EXPERIENCE

For women in the West, as frustrating as the remaining obstacles to influence may be, we actually have it pretty good. In much of the rest of the world, life for women is still a lot more difficult. Actually, life *for everyone* is a lot more difficult, and we shouldn't forget it. Alyse Nelson, CEO of the international women's leadership organization Vital Voices, wrote, "More than any title, rank or status, leadership is about the actions we take on a daily basis, the way we choose to live our lives, and the responsibility we take for the well being of the world we share."[6]

In Chapter Five, I introduced you to Loveleen Kacker, who moved from civil service into the nonprofit world in her home country of India. Loveleen was in a high-pressure job with a difficult boss when her parents fell ill. Bedridden, they needed home care, and because her brother lived abroad, the task fell solely to her. For two years, she juggled caring for them with keeping her demanding job. When they both passed away within four months of each other, she was grief stricken and drained. Then the will was read, and it was like a punch in the face. Everything went to her brother. In India, sons are valued more than daughters in a very literal way: because they carry on the family name, they are often sole recipients of the inheritance.

"To be discriminated against and denied my rights because of my gender was a shattering experience," says Loveleen. "I thought this was something that happened to other people, to the poor and uneducated, and certainly not to an empowered woman like me. But it did happen. It was gender discrimination at its worst, and the whole experience left me devastated and demoralized."

She could have fought her parents' will in court—in India, women are protected by the law but marginalized by the culture—but after sitting with her options, she realized that it wouldn't solve her problems. The real devastation she felt wasn't about money, but about the denial of her rights. In fact, a majority of the world's women do not legally own, control, or inherit property, land, or wealth.[7]

Loveleen explains her decision to become an activist, working to create opportunity and social justice for Indian women:

In India, every day women are discriminated against and treated as second-class citizens. Even today, the birth of a boy is celebrated while that of girl may be mourned. So I decided to do something about it. I quit my government job and moved into the social sector. I felt that I needed to fight for the cause of the poor and for the women. I took a role as the CEO of the foundation of one of India's most successful companies, Tech Mahindra, where I now work in the areas of education, vocational training, and disability. It is my mission to ensure that at least 50 percent of our beneficiaries are women and girls.

Consider thinking globally when it comes to finding ways of giving back. Karen Robinson Cope chairs the board of a microlending organization called Opportunity International, which helps four million women in the developing world each year start businesses. The average size of their first loan is $178, and with it comes a savings account, financial training, a support group, and life and business insurance.

"We're working with our sisters in the developing world to help them get their feet off the ground," says Karen. "Ninety-three percent of our loans go to women, and 95 percent of them get paid back. When you give a woman a loan for her business, what you find out is that once she is turning a profit, she spends her money on protein and education for her kids. So when you invest in a woman, you invest in a community." Our lives are so rich, and our potential for making a difference so great. Giving back is a responsibility to be honored and celebrated.

Loveleen and Karen have devoted themselves to making a difference. I'm not telling you their stories to humble you, although they may. I'm sharing them with you for two reasons: first, to remind you that we can't turn away from helping others even when the challenges are great, but second, to help you recognize the many blessings you already have.

Celebrate the sheer abundance of your life. It makes you want to do the most with what you have, and gives you the energy you need to swim against the current—to dare to pursue your vision with integrity, take smart risks, learn from failures, achieve with others, be gracious, and give back all along the way, enjoying every minute.

Go ahead, change life for us all. I dare you!

MORE ON THE MENTORS FEATURED IN *DARE*

Robin Bienfait, Former CIO, Research In Motion

In 2012 Robin retired from Research In Motion (RIM), where she had responsibility for overseeing the enterprise business unit, BlackBerry operations, and corporate IT. Before joining RIM, Robin held senior leadership positions within AT&T Labs and Global Network Services. She is a graduate of the Georgia Institute of Technology, with a master's degree in management of technology. Robin also holds a bachelor's degree in engineering from Central Missouri State University and an associate's degree in business from Maryland University–European Division. For more information, please visit www.RIM.com.

Roberta Bondar, Astronaut

Roberta is the world's first neurologist in space and Canada's first woman astronaut. After her mission, she headed an international space medicine research team, working with NASA for more than ten years. Recognition for her contributions to space medicine, engineering, and education include the NASA Space Medal; induction into the International Women's Forum Hall of Fame and the Canadian Medical Hall of Fame; officership in the Order of Canada and the Order of Ontario; twenty-four honorary doctorates from North American universities; the President's Award of the Council of Professional Engineers of Ontario; a star on Canada's Walk of Fame; and the Queen's Diamond Jubilee Medal. For more information, please visit www.robertabondar.com and the Web site for Roberta's foundation, www.therbf.org.

Genevieve Bos, CEO, IdeaString

Genevieve has started and sold multiple venture-backed and privately held corporations in the technology and media sector. She also cofounded *PINK* magazine and is a sought-after expert and speaker on professional success and entrepreneurship as they relate to women in business. Genevieve has a bachelor's degree from Georgia State University. For more information please visit www.www.genevievebos .com.

Molly Burke, Former General Counsel, GE Energy Services

Molly joined GE in July 1995 as a litigator at corporate headquarters, managing significant litigation across GE's business. Before joining GE she was a litigation partner in the Seattle office of Heller, Ehrman, White and McAuliffe, where she specialized in large commercial litigation. She is a graduate of Smith College and received her JD cum laude from Harvard Law School. For more information, please visit www.www.ge .com.

Anesa Chaibi, President and CEO, HD Supply Facilities Maintenance

Anesa began her career in 1989 in the GE Chemical and Materials Leadership Program. Since 2005, as president and CEO of HD Supply Facilities Maintenance, she has led transformational change, including acquisitions, integrations, divestures, and a major enterprise resource planning deployment. She has a bachelor's degree in chemical engineering from West Virginia University and an MBA from the Fuqua School of Business at Duke University. For more information, please visit www.hdsupply.com.

Anna Maria Chávez, CEO, Girl Scouts of the USA

Anna is a lifetime member of the Girl Scouts and an award-winning community leader. Prior to her current appointment, she served as CEO of Girl Scouts of Southwest Texas and as deputy chief of staff for urban relations and community development for the former governor of Arizona. She attended Yale University on a full scholarship and majored in history. After graduation she served as a law clerk in Arizona, and then attended the University of Arizona Law School. For more information, please visit www.girlscouts.org.

Tena Clark, CEO and Chief Creative Officer, DMI Music and Media Solutions

Tena, among the most influential women in American media, founded DMI fifteen years ago. An award-willing songwriter and one of the rare female producers in the music business, she has contributed to multi-platinum movie soundtracks as well as television shows and commercials. DMI is at the forefront of entertainment and music marketing, crafting strategies and activations for global brands that include Build-A-Bear, Cisco, Delta Air Lines, and General Mills. Tena is a graduate the University of Southern Mississippi. For more information, please visit www.dmimusic.com.

Kat Cole, President, Cinnabon

Kat has served as the president of Cinnabon since January 2011, having previously served as chief operating officer. She is responsible for overseeing more than 770 franchised locations worldwide. Prior to her role at Cinnabon, Kat was vice president of Hooters of America. She is an active board member of the Women's Food Service Forum and an accomplished motivational speaker and author. She is an avid volunteer with organizations that support women and children and fight hunger and homelessness. She attended the University of North Florida and received her MBA from Georgia State University. For more information, please visit www.cinnabon.com

Karen Robinson Cope, SVP of Sales and Marketing, NanoLumens

Karen is a serial entrepreneur who has been CEO of four angel or venture-backed companies over the last twenty years. She is one of a handful of women who have raised over $75 million in the Southeast and successfully built and sold multiple companies. A graduate of the University of Redlands, Karen has received a number of national and international honors and awards, and is a frequent speaker at both the local and national levels. For more information, please visit www.nanolumens.com.

Diana Einterz, Head of Americas, Orange Business Services

Diana has extensive global telecommunications industry experience. At Orange she was previously head of regional operations and led a team of more than 2,100 technicians and support staff, delivering services to multinational corporations in over 220 countries and territories. Before joining Orange she served in a variety of executive posts at AT&T, overseeing the maintenance and provisioning of the telecom provider's domestic and international networks. Diana has a bachelor's degree in mathematics and computer science from McGill University. For more information, please visit www.orange-business.com.

Susan Grant, Executive VP, CNN News Services

Under Susan's stewardship, CNN Digital has become the Internet's leading news destination globally. Also included in her portfolio of businesses are CNNMoney.com, CNN Mobile, and CNN iReport. In 2008 the Radio and Television News Directors Association honored Susan with its First Amendment Service Award. She serves on the board of directors for Internet Broadcasting; the board of trustees for the Morehouse School of Medicine; the board of visitors for Agnes Scott College; and the board of Heifer International, a nonprofit, humanitarian organization dedicated to ending hunger and poverty and caring for the earth. Susan is a graduate of Vassar College. For more information, please visit www.cnn.com.

Kim Greene, President and CEO, Southern Company Services

Kim has an extensive background in the electric utility industry. She served as the executive vice president and chief generation officer of the Tennessee Valley Authority prior to being selected as president and CEO, in which capacity she oversees the shared services of Southern Company's $18 billion enterprise. She holds degrees from the University of Tennessee in engineering sciences and mechanics, the University of Alabama–Birmingham in biomedical engineering, and Samford University in business administration. She also attended the Advanced Management Program at Harvard Business School. For more information, please visit www.southerncompany.com.

Jeanette Horan, CIO, IBM

Jeanette was appointed CIO of IBM in May 2011. She is responsible for driving IBM's transformation initiative and equipping IBMers with the technology and tools they need to better support clients and achieve IBM's objectives. She joined IBM in 1998 and has held numerous leadership positions across the enterprise. Before joining IBM she spent four years at Digital Equipment Corporation. She has more than twenty-five years of experience in development and management roles in the computer industry. She has a bachelor's degree in mathematics from the University of London and an MBA from Boston University. For more information, please visit www.ibm.com.

Rebecca Jacoby, CIO and SVP, IT and Cloud & Systems Management Technology Group, Cisco

Rebecca's extensive understanding of business operations, infrastructure, and application deployments as well as her knowledge of products, software, and services help her advance Cisco's business through the use of Cisco technology. Since joining Cisco in 1995 she has held a variety of leadership roles in operations, manufacturing, and IT. Prior to joining Cisco, she held numerous planning and operations positions at other companies in Silicon Valley. She holds a bachelor's degree in economics from the University of the Pacific and a master's degree in business administration from Santa Clara University. For more information, please visit www.cisco.com.

Loveleen Kacker, CEO, Tech Mahindra Foundation

Loveleen spent the first thirty years of her career working as a civil servant, acting in various capacities in the Indian government. She voluntarily retired from the government to take on her current role. The Tech Mahindra Foundation is the corporate social responsibility wing of Tech Mahindra, an IT outsourcing company. In addition to her work with the foundation, she is a published writer of fiction, with sixteen books to her credit. She has a master's degree in political science and a PhD in social anthropology. For more information, please visit www.techmahindrafoundation.org.

Adriana Karaboutis, VP and Global CIO, Dell

Adriana is responsible for managing an innovative global IT enterprise focused on technology breakthroughs for Dell and its customers. Before coming to Dell, she spent over twenty years in the auto industry in various leadership positions within IT and business operations as global manufacturing and labor information officer of General Motors. She received a bachelor's degree in computer science from Wayne State University, where she was a Merit Scholar, and where she subsequently pursued graduate electronic computer control systems studies. For more information, please visit www.dell.com.

Penny Manuel, Former Executive VP of Engineering and Construction Services, Southern Company

Penny was responsible for overseeing new power generation, environmental strategy development, major project design and construction execution, technology due diligence, and operations and maintenance support for Southern Company. She began her career with Southern Company in 1982 as an engineer, and later moved into senior management and executive positions. Penny has a bachelor's degree in materials engineering from the University of Alabama at Birmingham and has completed the Advanced Management Program at Harvard Business School. For more information, please visit www.southerncompany.com.

Kathleen Matthews, Chief Communications and Public Affairs Officer, Marriott International

Kathleen is responsible for Marriott's global brand, public relations, corporate communications, social responsibility, and government affairs. She serves on the U.S. Travel and Tourism Advisory Board to the Secretary of Commerce. Prior to her career at Marriott, she was an award-winning news anchor at the ABC-TV affiliate in Washington DC and hosted the nationally syndicated *Working Woman* television show. She is a 1975 graduate of Stanford University and was a 2004 Fellow at the Institute of Politics at the Kennedy School of Government at Harvard University. For more information, please visit www.marriott.com.

Lyn McDermid, CIO, Federal Reserve System

Lyn became chief information officer for the Federal Reserve System in 2012, after she retired as senior vice president and chief information officer of Dominion Resources, a $15 billion power and energy company. At Dominion, she led an organization of 1,200 people, overseeing all IT activities. During the course of her career, Lyn has been included in *Computerworld*'s list of "Premier 100 IT Leaders" and has received the Executive Women in Business Achievement Award. Lyn is a graduate of Mary Baldwin College and received her master's degree from the University of Richmond. For more information, please visit www.richmondfed.org.

Martha McGill, Chief Operating Officer, Miami Children's Hospital

Martha is responsible for overseeing operations of Miami Children's Hospital, a 289-bed pediatric hospital with nine ambulatory care centers—the region's only health care system exclusively for children. Prior to this role, she was senior vice president of operations for Children's Healthcare of Atlanta, where she served for twenty-three years. Martha is a graduate of the Valdosta State University College of Nursing and earned master's degrees in health care administration and business administration from Georgia State University. For more information, please visit www.mch.com.

Penny McIntyre, Former President, Consumer Group, Newell Rubbermaid

Penny has over twenty years of experience at premier consumer packaged goods companies, including Newell Rubbermaid, the Coca-Cola Company, and SC Johnson. She has led businesses globally, leveraging her skills in general management, marketing, and talent development. At Newell Rubbermaid she was responsible for a $3.2 billion business unit with ten thousand people worldwide. She led the Rubbermaid, Sharpie, Calphalon, Levolor, Paper Mate, and Parker businesses, all leaders in their respective categories. Peggy is a graduate of the Ivey Business School at the University of Western Ontario, and has been honored with various awards related to her work as an advocate for women, including the YWCA's Woman of Achievement award. For more information, please visit www.newellrubbermaid.com.

Hala Moddelmog, President, Arby's

Hala was the first woman to lead an international restaurant company. In 1995 she was named president of Church's Chicken. In 2006 she was named president and CEO of Susan G. Komen for the Cure, the world's largest grassroots network dedicated to eradicating breast cancer. She was named to her current position in 2010. She is also chairman of the Arby's Foundation and is focused on ending childhood hunger in America. She serves on the board of Amerigroup and is a strong advocate for increasing women's participation on public boards. Hala is a graduate of Georgia Southern University, having received a degree in fine arts and English and a master of arts in journalism and mass communications from the University of Georgia. For more information, please visit www.discoverarbys.com.

Anne Mulcahy, Former Chairman and CEO, Xerox Corporation

In addition to her former roles as chairman, CEO, and board member of Xerox, Anne has served on the boards of Catalyst, Citigroup, Fuji Xerox Company, and Target Corporation. She was selected as CEO of the Year in 2008 by *Chief Executive* magazine. Anne joined Xerox in 1976 as a field sales representative and rose through the ranks. She is a graduate of Marymount College, where she received a BA in English and journalism. For more information, please visit www.xerox.com.

Joan Pertak, SVP and CIO, PepsiCo Americas Beverages and Quaker Foods and Snacks in North America

Joan has twenty-five years of PepsiCo experience in the areas of supply chain and business and information solutions. Before joining PepsiCo she was a technical consultant and a retail manager. She is the executive sponsor of the Business and Information Solutions Mentoring Program and an executive sponsor of the EQUAL employee resource group, which supports PepsiCo's gay, lesbian, bisexual, and transgender employees. She is also an adviser to PepsiCo's Women's Inclusion Network. She is a graduate of the State University of New York at Albany. For more information, please visit www.pepsico.com.

Veronica Sheehan, SVP, Global Network Operations and International IT, Turner Broadcasting System

Veronica joined Turner Broadcasting System (TBS) in 1999 as director of broadcast operations and has served in many executive leadership roles. In her current role she has oversight of U.S. network operations and international network operations and IT in the Latin America, Asia Pacific, Europe, and Middle East Africa regions. She is the founding chair of the TBS business resource group Turner Women Today. She has won numerous awards, including being recognized as one of the most powerful women in technology by *CableWorld* magazine. Most recently she was awarded Mother of the Year 2011 by *Working Mother* magazine. She earned a bachelor's degree in communications and journalism at St. John Fisher College in Rochester, New York. For more information, please visit www.turner.com.

Betty Siegel, President Emeritus, Kennesaw State University

Betty was the first female president of the University System of Georgia and served in that position for twenty-five years, making her the longest-serving female president of a state university in the United States. Under her leadership, Kennesaw grew from four thousand to eighteen thousand students. She continues to serve Kennesaw State University as president emeritus, and the world as an endowed chair of the Siegel Institute for Leadership, Ethics and Character. She received her bachelor's degree from Wake Forest, a master's degree from the University of North Carolina, and a PhD in education from Florida State University. She also undertook postdoctoral studies at Indiana University. She holds five honorary doctorates. For more information, please visit www.kennesaw.edu.

Beverly Daniel Tatum, President, Spelman College

Beverly has served as the president of Spelman College since 2002. She is recognized as a race relations expert and is the author of several books. Prior to 2002 she spent thirteen years at Mount Holyoke College as professor, dean, and acting president. She is also a corporate director of Georgia Power. She holds a BA in psychology from Wesleyan University, an MA and PhD in clinical psychology from the University of Michigan, and an MA in religious studies form Hartford Seminary. For more information, please visit www.spelman.edu.

Carol B. Tomé, CFO and Executive VP of Corporate Services, The Home Depot

Carol joined The Home Depot in 1995 and has served in her current role since 2001. She provides leadership in the areas of real estate, store construction, financial services, strategic business development, and growth initiatives. Prior to her role at the Home Depot, she was vice president and treasurer of Riverwood International Corporation. She serves as a corporate director at UPS and is chair of its audit committee. She was the chair of the board of the Federal Reserve Bank of Atlanta and a key leader in the Atlanta civic community. She holds a bachelor's degree in communication from the University of Wyoming and a master's degree in business administration in finance from the University of Denver. For more information, please visit www.homedepot.com.

Lora G. Weiss, Lab Chief Scientist and Technical Director of Autonomous Systems, Georgia Tech Research Institute

Lora's research is on the design and development of robots and unmanned systems. She has conducted research on air, ground, sea-surface, and undersea robotic systems. She has served on the board of directors for the Association for Unmanned Vehicle Systems International, on the Technical Advisory Board of the Nation's Robotics Technology Consortium, and as an Executive Board Member of the National Defense Industrial Association. She currently chairs the American Society for Testing and Materials Committee on Unmanned Maritime Vehicle Autonomy and Control. Lora has a BS in mathematics from Boston University, a master's in mathematics from UCLA, and a PhD in acoustical engineering from Penn State. For more information, please visit http://robotics.gatech.edu.

NOTES

Introduction

1. Bureau of Labor Statistics. "Table 11: Employed Persons by Detailed Occupation, Sex, Race, and Hispanic or Latino Ethnicity," Current Population Survey. [http://www.bls.gov/cps/cpsaat11.pdf]. *Annual Averages 2012*. 2013, 1; Bureau of Labor Statistics. "Table 3: Employment Status of the Civilian Noninstitutional Population by Age, Sex, and Race," Current Population Survey. [http://www.bls.gov/cps/cpsaat03.htm]. *Annual Averages 2012*. 2013.

2. Soares, Rachel, Bonaparte, Samantha, Campbell, Sherika, Margolin, Vicky, and Spencer, Jocelyn. "2012 Catalyst Census: Fortune 500 Women Executive Officers and Top Earners." Catalyst, 2012; Soares, Rachel, Cobb, Baye, Lebow, Ellen, Winsten, Hannah, Wojnas, Veronica, and Regis, Allyson. "2011 Catalyst Census: Fortune 500 Women Executive Officers and Top Earners." Catalyst, 2011.

3. Homan, Timothy R. "Fewer Nations Made Progress to Close Gender Gap: Study." [http://www.bloomberg.com/news/2011–11–01/fewer-nations-made-progress-on-reducing-gender-gap-study-says.html]. November 1, 2011.

4. Barsh, Joanna, and Yee, Lareina. "Unlocking the Full Potential of Women in the U.S. Economy." [http://www.mckinsey.com/

205

client_service/organization/latest_thinking/unlocking_the_ full_potential]. April 2011.

Chapter 1

1. Catalyst. "Different Cultures, Similar Perceptions: Stereotyping of Western European Business Leaders." [http://www.catalyst .org/knowledge/different-cultures-similar-perceptions-stereo- typing-western-european-business-leaders]. June 13, 2006.

2. Barsh, Joanna, and Yee, Lareina. "Unlocking the Full Potential of Women in the U.S. Economy." [http://www.mckinsey.com/ client_service/organization/latest_thinking/unlocking_the_ full_potential]. April 2011.

3. Ibid.

4. "About Spelman College." [http://www.spelman.edu/about- us]. n.d.

5. Liswood, Laura. *Women World Leaders: Fifteen Great Politicians Tell Their Story.* New York, NY: New York University Press, 1996.

6. Halvorson, Heidi Grant. *Succeed: How We Can Reach Our Goals.* New York, NY: Hudson Street Press, 2011.

Chapter 2

1. Buckley, Peter, personal interview with Rebecca Blalock, Octo- ber 8, 2012.

2. Ferrazzi, Keith. *Who's Got Your Back.* New York, NY: Crown Business, 2009, 89.

Chapter 3

1. "Executive Summary: The 2013 Edelman Trust Barometer." [http://www.scribd.com/doc/121501475/Executive-Summary- 2013-Edelman-Trust-Barometer]. January 2013.

2. Friedman, Thomas L. "Average Is Over." [http://www.nytimes .com/2012/01/25/opinion/friedman-average-is-over.html]. *The New York Times.* January 24, 2012.

3. Bureau of Labor Statistics. "Table A-7: Time Spent in Primary Activities by Married Mothers and Fathers with Own Household Children Under 18 by Employment Status of Self and Spouse and Age of Youngest Child, Average for the Combined Years 2007–11," American Time Use Survey. [http://www.bls.gov/ tus/tables/a7_0711.htm]. 2011.

4. Branstiter, Heather, Glick, Peter, Johnson, Cathryn, and Larsen, Sadie. "Evaluations of Sexy Women in Low- and High-Status Jobs." *Psychology of Women Quarterly.* December 2005, Vol. 29, No. 4, 389–395.

5. Babcock, Linda, and Laschever, Susan. *Women Don't Ask: Negotiation and the Gender Divide.* Princeton, NJ: Princeton University Press, 2003, 114.

6. Brown, Steve. *How to Talk So People Will Listen.* Grand Rapids, MI: Baker Books, 1993, 72.

Chapter 4

1. "The Quotable Thatcher: 15 of Her Best Quips." [http://worldnews.nbcnews.com/_news/2013/04/08/17654349-the-quotable-thatcher-15-of-her-best-quips?lite]. April 8, 2013.

2. Tannen, Deborah. *You Just Don't Understand: Women and Men in Conversation.* New York, NY: HarperCollins, 1990.

3. Valenti, Jessica. "She Who Dies with the Most 'Likes' Wins?" [http://www.thenation.com/blog/171520/she-who-dies-most-likes-wins#]. November 29, 2012.

4. Martin, Joanne. "Gender-Related Material in the New Core Curriculum." [http://www.gsb.stanford.edu/news/headlines/wim_martin07.shtml]. January 1, 2007.

5. Stoop, David. *You Are What You Think* (Spire edition). Grand Rapids, MI: Revell, 2003, 30–31.

6. Hanson, Rick, with Mendius, Richard. *Buddha's Brain: The Practical Neuroscience of Happiness, Love, and Wisdom.* Oakland, CA: New Harbinger, 2009, 41.

7. Seligman, Martin E. P. *Learned Optimism: How to Change Your Mind and Your Life.* New York, NY: Vintage/Random House, 2006

8. Gottman, John. *Why Marriages Succeed or Fail: And How You Can Make Yours Last.* New York, NY: Simon and Schuster, 1995.

9. Clance, Pauline Rose, and Imes, Suzanne. "The Imposter Phenomenon in High Achieving Women: Dynamics and Therapeutic Intervention." [http://www.paulineroseclance.com/pdf/ip_high_achieving_women.pdf]. *Psychotherapy Theory, Research and Practice.* Fall 1978, Vol. 15, No. 3.

10. Dweck, Carol. *Mindset: The New Psychology of Success*. New York, NY: Ballantine Books, 2006, 5.
11. Ibid., 6.
12. Christakis, Nicholas A., and Fowler, James H. *Connected: The Surprising Power of Our Social Networks*. New York, NY: Little, Brown, 2009.
13. Hanson, with Mendius, *Buddha's Brain*.

Chapter 5

1. Raz, Tahl. "The Social Capitalist," podcast episode featuring John Hagel and John Seely Brown. [https://itunes.apple.com/us/podcast/social-capitalist-podcast/id544031855]. Ferrazzi Greenlight, February 2012.
2. Ferrazzi, Keith. *Who's Got Your Back*. New York, NY: Crown Business, 2009, 76.

Chapter 6

1. Sundheim, Doug. "Do Women Take as Many Risks as Men?" [http://blogs.hbr.org/cs/2013/02/do_women_take_as_many_risks_as.html]. February 27, 2013.
2. Harari, Oren. *The Powell Principles: 24 Lessons from Colin Powell*. New York, NY: McGraw-Hill, 2003, 30.
3. Ibid., 3.
4. Newton, James D. *Uncommon Friends: Life with Thomas Edison, Henry Ford, Harvey Firestone, Alexis Carrel and Charles Lindbergh*. New York, NY: Mariner Books, 1987, 24.
5. Buckley, Peter, personal interview with Rebecca Blalock, October 8, 2012.

Chapter 7

1. Barsh, Joanna, and Yee, Lareina. "Unlocking the Full Potential of Women in the U.S. Economy." [http://www.mckinsey.com/client_service/organization/latest_thinking/unlocking_the_full_potential]. April 2011.
2. Flynn, Francis J., and Lake, Vanessa K. B. "If You Need Help, Just Ask: Underestimating Compliance with Direct Requests for Help." *Journal of Personal and Social Psychology*. July 2008, Vol. 95, No. 1, 128–143.

3. Barsh and Yee, "Unlocking the Full Potential."

4. Ferrazzi, Keith. *Who's Got Your Back.* New York, NY: Crown Business, 2009.

Chapter 8

1. Martin, Chuck. *Coffee at Luna's: A Business Fable.* Boston, MA: NFI Research, 2005.

2. Covey, Stephen. *The Speed of Trust.* New York, NY: Free Press, 2006.

Chapter 9

1. "Why Do You Think There Aren't More Women CEO's?" [www.linkedin.com/osview/why.do.you.think.there.aren't.more.women.ceo's]. April 14, 2013.

2. Cartner, Nancy M., Dinolfo, Sarah, and Silva, Christine. "High Potentials in the Pipeline: Leaders Pay It Forward." [http://www.catalyst.org/knowledge/high-potentials-pipeline-leaders-pay-it-forward]. Catalyst, 2012.

3. Ibid.

4. "Paying It Forward Pays Back for Business Leaders: Developing Others Pays Off in Career Growth—And Reveals No Queen Bees Here, Catalyst Study Finds," press release. [http://www.catalyst.org/media/paying-it-forward-pays-back-business-leaders].

5. Holincheck, James. "Case Study: Workforce Analytics at Sun." [http://www.gartner.com/id=497507]. Gartner Research, October 2006.

6. Nelson, Alyse. *Vital Voices: The Power of Women Leading Change Around the World.* San Francisco, CA: Jossey-Bass, 2012, xxiii.

7. Benschop, Marjolein. "Women's Rights to Land and Property." [http://www.unhabitat.org/downloads/docs/1556_72513_CSDWomen.pdf]. Commission on Sustainable Development, April 2004.

ACKNOWLEDGMENTS

I have many people to thank for helping make this book a reality. First and foremost is Sara Grace, who served as my editor—I could not have been more satisfied with our collaboration. I also thank Alan Axelrod for his gifted editing and coaching during the early stages of this project. Finally, the experience, insights, and polish brought by Karen Murphy and John Maas at Jossey-Bass made this book a better product. I am grateful for their commitment to excellence, and for their pushing me to go the distance.

I want to thank my friends who diligently read and provided feedback as I drafted early versions of this book. This includes Pam Host, Judy Maloney, Karen Robinson Cope, Evelyn Bailey, Jim Barber, Laura Butts, Chris St. Clare, Molly Burke, Henna Inam, Lalita Valvalli, Vish Narendra, Ally Sheintal Dobbs, Bob Steed, and Susan Hitchcock. Only true friends would invest such time and effort in helping me create a great experience for readers.

There are numerous senior executive women who shared their insights and wisdom with me. Chief among them is Anne Mulcahy, who did not hesitate when I asked her to write the foreword. Anyone who says women don't help other women has never experienced an outpouring of support as I did from my female friends as I wrote this book. I am especially grateful to the incredibly generous women who agreed to let me share their insights and contributed profiles, the source of many valuable lessons in *Dare*: Robin Bienfait, Roberta Bondar, Genevieve Bos, Molly Burke, Anesa Chaibi, Anna Maria Chávez, Tena Clark, Kat Cole, Karen Robinson Cope, Diana Einterz, Susan Grant, Kim Greene, Jeanette Horan, Rebecca Jacoby, Loveleen Kacker, Adriana Karaboutis, Penny Manuel, Kathleen Matthews, Lyn McDermid, Martha McGill, Penny McIntyre, Hala Moddelmog, Joan Pertak, Veronica Sheehan, Betty Siegel, Beverly Daniel Tatum, Carol B. Tomé, and Lora G. Weiss. We can learn much from these great and wise role models. I also want to acknowledge others who provided input, counsel, connections, and support. This list of terrific women includes Susan Bell, Donna Henderson, Ann Stallard, Elisabeth Kiss, Elisabeth Marchant, Leslie Sibert, Marilyn Wright, Pat Upshaw Monteith, Annie Hunt Burriss, Susan Stautberg, Janice Rys, Shan Cooper, Beverly Langford, Patti Gilmer, Meredith Hodges, Mary Parker, Kris Spain, Linda Rogers, Mahvash Yazdi, Gail Evans, Bobbie Batista, Erika Alexander, Sandy Hofmann, Lousie Wells, Maria Cibel, Renata Shore, Barbara Gunn, Cynthia Goode, Lori Oliver, Mary Ellen Garrett, Martha Brooks, Alicia Philipp, Aline Ward, Sharon Lechter, Mylle Mangum, Lynne Ellyn, Jackie McKinley, Marilyn Midyette, Robin Spratlin, Sherry McGill Quinn, Carey White, Sarah O'Brien, Cindy Carter, Diane Homesley, Juanita Baranco, Donna Buchanan, Marie Mouchet, Elena Mappus, Jeannice Hall, Laura Liswood, Helene Lollis, Caren Byrd, Susan Bernstein, Carrie Wheeler, Jean Holley, Paula Staggs, Tracy Crump, Meg Reggie, and Kathy Amechee.

Amanda Brown-Olmstead has been a great mentor throughout my career and helped coach and counsel me through the creation of this book. Brie McKeller is a master project manager. Her strategic thinking and drive have been tremendous assets in promoting and marketing the book. Sean Young has been instrumental in leveraging technology and social media to extend the reach of the book. Thanks to the brilliant Peter Buckley of Georgia Regents University for providing psychological background for the book. Thanks also to some remarkably supportive men who provided great counsel and contacts, including Frank McCloskey; Ricky Steele; Jeff Rosensweig; Arvind Malhotra; David Connell; Matt Caughey; Bill Dahlberg; Ben Hendrick; John Yates; Victor Inzunza; Heath Nash; Ross Mason; and, of course, my dad, Bill Bradford. I am very grateful to my agent, Ed Claflin, for his tireless work on my behalf.

I want to thank Bonnie Daneker, who believed in me and encouraged me to put my thoughts on paper. I'm not certain I would have embarked on this journey without her push in this direction.

I reserve my final thank you for my husband, Jim Blalock, and our daughter, Alex. They have been here to help me through the many twists and turns of my career and cheered me on from the sidelines as I wrote this book. I can't imagine what life would be like without them. I am a blessed woman, indeed.

Becky Blalock
Atlanta, Georgia

Becky Blalock is a veteran of the corporate world. She began her career at Southern Company, an $18 billion corporation and one of the nation's largest utility companies, in 1979, where she rose to become senior vice president and chief information officer before retiring in 2011. In addition to her work in IT, she held leadership positions in accounting, finance, marketing, corporate communications, external affairs, and customer service—often as the first woman in the company to do so. Becky is a partner with Advisory Capital, where she provides strategic consulting, and serves on the boards of companies involved in energy, information technology, and medicine.

A sought-after speaker, Becky has long been recognized as a thought leader in the IT and utility industries. *Energy Biz* magazine named her CIO of the Year in 2009, *Computer World* magazine named her a Premier IT Leader, and she is listed in the *Who's Who in Science and Engineering*. An advocate for women and children, she is a member of the YWCA's Academy of Women Achievers and was presented with the Shining Star Award from the Atlanta Women's Foundation.

Becky has a master's degree from Mercer University and a bachelor's degree in business from the University of West

Georgia. She completed the Program for Management Development at Harvard University.

She lives in Atlanta, Georgia, with her husband, Jim, and *Dare* is her first book. For more information, please visit www .beckyblalock.com.

INDEX

Feedback: accepting graciously, 40; asking for, 32–34; eliciting candid, 36–38; evaluating and considering, 38–39; giving constructive, 38; handling critical, 36; learning from, 28, 31, 98, 166–167; listening to, 172–173; requesting when denied raise, 61; using storytelling in, 69
Ferrazzi, Keith, 33, 105, 155, 157
First impressions, 55
First Law of Motion (Newton), 156
Fixed mind-sets, 87–88
Flynn, Frank, 80
Fowler, James, 90
Franklin, Benjamin, 127
Friendships: developing, 135; importance of, 132; listening within, 171–174
Fun, 26

G
Gallup, 33
Gartner Research, 180
Gender bias: countering with mentoring, 189–190; daring to overcome, 8–10; demonstrated in "Heidi/Howard" experiment, 80; examples of international, 190–193; overcoming corporate, 144–147; pay raises and, 59–61; seeking advice from women mentors, 147; views of risk taking, 118–119
Georgia Power Company, 1
Giving, 26
Goals: adapting and pursuing, 16, 18; aligning with values, 21–22, 26; developing visionary, 15; writing down, 94
Grant, Susan, 27–28, 198
Gratitude, 92
Greene, Kim, 117, 170–171, 198

Growth: as core value, 26; mind-sets for, 87–88

H
Hagel, John, 104
Halvorson, Heidi Grant, 21
Handshakes, 142
Harmonizing core values with goals, 22
Health: benefits of personal, 92; protecting personal, 53–54
Heart of Networking, The (Steele), 142
"Heidi/Howard" experiment, 80
Helping others: becoming role model, 177–178; benefits of, 179–181; creating environment for, 189–190; early in career, 188; failures when, 185–186; finding protégés, 184–186; improving leadership by, 182–183; informally vs. formally, 185; making time for, 190; paying it forward, 9–10
Home Depot, 22–23
Horan, Jeanette, 102, 107, 151, 198–199

I
Imes, Suzanne, 86
Imposter syndrome, 85–87
Inertia in relationships, 156
Informal mentoring, 145, 185
Inspiration: feedback engendering, 38; making communications with, 167
Integrity: being true to self, 28; identifying core values, 21–24; importance of, 26; making personal brand, 44–46, 143; reliability and, 52–53; reputation for results and, 46–48; upholding personal, 23–25
Intuition, 112–113, 120